PRAISE FOR *FREE MONEY*

"Austin L. Church has penned a game-changer. In Free Money, he unpacks the art and science of pricing for freelancers and shares a treasure trove of relatable examples and anecdotes. This book offers not only a path to better income but also a better relationship with money and a better life. Every page resonates with wisdom and practicality. Prepare to be transformed."
—**Ed Gandia**, Founder, High-Income Business Writing

"This book is perfect for freelancers – it will get you through, over and past any money blocks you have, thanks to a combination of the clarity Austin brings, the stories he tells and the lilt of his southern voice, which you can literally hear on the page. He even makes the math painless – almost! Highly recommended reading!"
—**Ilise Benun**, Founder of Marketing-Mentor.com and Author of *The Creative Professional's Guide to Money* and *The Simplest Marketing Plan*

"If you want to make more money as a freelancer or consultant, buy this book and do what it says."
—**Tim Stoddart**, Partner, Copyblogger

"For a long time, talking about money has been taboo. But freelancers need to understand money and pricing in order to build a business that supports their lifestyle (rather than destroys it). Free Money is essential reading for freelancers who truly want to take control of their time."
—**Jay Clouse**, Founder of Freelancing School & Creator Science Lab

"Have you ever told a potential client your price and immediately thought 'Oh gosh, was that too much? Not enough? What have I done?!' Congratulations, you're normal—but after reading Free Money you'll have a super smart pricing strategy so you never feel or think that again."

—**John Meese**, Author of *Survive and Thrive* & *Always Be Teaching*

"Austin is the #1 expert on freelance pricing. Also, what's 'freelance'?"

—**Austin's Mom**

A Guide to Pricing Your Services So You Can Unlock a Better Lifestyle

FREE MONEY

Nine Counterintuitive Moves for Life-Changing Freelance Income

AUSTIN L. CHURCH

© 2024 Austin L. Church All rights reserved. No part of this book may be reproduced by any mechanical, photographic, or electronic process, or in the form of phonographic recording; nor may it be stored in a retrieval system, transmitted, or otherwise copied for public or private use—other than for "fair use" as brief quotations embodied in articles and reviews—without prior written permission of the author.

The author of this book does not dispense business advice, only offers information of a general nature. This book is not intended to be a definitive guide or to replace advice from a qualified professional. Business of any kind involves risk. There is no guarantee that the methods suggested in this book will work for you. In the event that you use any of the information or methods described in this book, the author and publisher assume no responsibility for your actions and assume no liability for any losses that you may sustain. Any such responsibility or liability is expressly disclaimed.

TILT PUBLISHING

700 Park Offices Drive, Suite 250
Research Triangle, NC 27709

ISBN: 979-8-9890257-0-1 (Paperback)
ISBN: 979-8-9890257-1-8 (Hardcover))

DISCLAIMER

You'll be shocked to know I'm not a tax professional, financial expert, accountant, debt counselor, or lion tamer. I lack the qualifications to give financial or tax advice, so I don't give financial advice.

Everything in this book is for informational purposes only.

I can't tell you how to invest your money, pay off your debt, or execute a double fiscal somersault. Please consult with a tax professional, and while you're at it, ask them to explain the difference between tax avoidance and tax evasion.

Throughout the book I use examples and scenarios I'm familiar with as a US citizen. However, I've done my best to tease out timeless principles that apply no matter where you live.

*To my wife, Megan Pearl, who sees the best in me
and reminds me to do the same*

CONTENTS

INTRODUCTION:
Desperation Was the Real Creator — 9

PART I: PRICING

MOVE ONE:
Find Your Survival Number — 21

MOVE TWO:
Find Your True Availability — 33

MOVE THREE:
Find Your Survival Rate, Dream Number, and Dream Rate — 43

MOVE FOUR:
Set Your Pessimistic Price — 55

PART II: EARNING

MOVE FIVE:
Find Your Next Three — 75

MOVE SIX:
Change Your Mind — 107

MOVE SEVEN:
Take Your Vitamins — 154

MOVE EIGHT:
Get Answers — 202

MOVE NINE:
Run Victory Laps — 224

CONCLUSION — 238

APPENDIX — 242

NOTES — 284

ACKNOWLEDGEMENTS — 295

"I wish I had charged less in the past."

—No Freelancer Ever

INTRODUCTION:

Desperation Was the Real Creator

THE BEACH IS THE WORST PLACE FOR A CRISIS, DON'T YOU THINK?

In September 2015, my family of four was vacationing with friends on St. George Island in Florida. Everything went great at first: sunshine, Apalachicola oysters, and our precious babies covered in sugary sand.

At one point, I snuck away to do some admin work and pay bills. When I logged into my checking and credit card accounts, I got a punch to the gut. My wife and I didn't have enough cash in checking to pay off the credit card in full.

That credit card balance might seem like a small thing, but for me, it signified history repeating. When we had paid off the last of our wedding expenses, student loans, and credit card debt back in August 2013, I'd felt so proud. We'd taken a trip to Las Vegas to celebrate, and I'd had several $20,000 and $30,000 months since then. That surplus had enabled me to invest $25,000 in a tech startup.

Closeup.fm had done what hungry startups do and consumed most of my time and attention. The trouble was, the company couldn't afford to pay me or my cofounder, and there weren't enough hours left over to find and fulfill the freelance projects I still relied on to pay my family's bills. Our family had grown, and I hadn't raised my rates in two-and-a-half years. I was so preoccupied with incubators, accelerators, and investors, I hadn't stayed in touch with past clients. I was working long hours without getting ahead. I was at a loss, metaphorically and financially.

I didn't have a full-on panic attack at the kitchen table in that beach rental, but as I stared at those two account balances, one too small and the other too big, the reality I'd shoved to the periphery came crashing in. All the anxiety, self-doubt, and shame knocked me over like one of the waves I could hear outside. I felt like a failure as a husband and father.

Have you ever had a low point like that when you couldn't stop thinking about a situation? You needed to snap out of it, but your mind was a skater at an ice rink. It went in circles while the same worn-out track blared from the speakers. The chorus of my track went like this: *How could I have been so stupid? How could I have made so many mistakes? How are we below zero again?*

Delightful travel companion that I am, I spent the rest of the "vacation" overhauling my pricing instead of being fully present for my family and friends.

I'd never thought deeply about my approach to pricing, and when I started searching online, the advice and processes I found had gaping holes. Wasn't it obvious that freelancers must strategically price and plan for fatter months to cover leaner ones and any time off, too? Unlike nine-to-five employees, we don't get paid vacations.

And what about the fact that no freelancer can bill clients forty or more hours for weeks and months on end? It's not realistic to bill out more than 70 percent of your working hours for any length of time. You either burn yourself out or guarantee a dry spell because you invested no time on marketing. Admin, the business itself, and the rest of our lives all deserve attention, too. What we charge must account for all this non-billable time.

In *Republic*, Plato writes, "Our need will be the real creator." In my case, "desperation" was the "need." I had to start charging prices that made sense for my family's financial needs, and I had to invent the process for setting those prices because the one I needed didn't exist. My cute little crisis planted the seed for this book.

Do you need a breakthrough with your pricing?

Presumably, you're reading this book because you want to rethink what you charge. You may have experienced an inciting incident which looks different based on where you are on the freelance journey.

Maybe you're a *Moonlighter* who freelances on the side. You don't rely on your freelance income—at least not yet—so when Bobby Boogerface, executive director of a nonprofit and King of Pointless Meetings, promised to make up for his itty-bitty budget by being easy to work with, you believed him. Later, when he spoiled your lunch hour with yet another pointless call, you decided enough was enough. You may have a nine-to-five job, but you still need to charge like a full-time freelancer.

Maybe you're a *Hustler* working hard and smart to replace the salary at your last job. Inez, founder of a confusing but grandiose startup, hired you for a visual identity project. Your enthusiasm dissipated when you realized that Inez didn't want a strategic partner. No, she wanted a design puppet and person-shaped paintbrush. You should have known that "I'm not worried about the price" meant "I'm going to henpeck you to death with silly changes." Clearly, you need prices that position you as the authority. An "affordable" hourly rate ain't cutting it.

Maybe you're a *Lifestyler* who has already learned how to navigate the rowdy realm of Freelance. But recently, you've drifted too close to the border of Burnout. You're feeling a little lost and turned around and could use a well-drawn map for finding Satisfaction—that is, making the same income in less time.

Maybe you're a *Diversifier* who is doing well financially, thank you very much. But you're starting to think beyond freelancing. Should you scale up into a lean agency? Or maybe sell advice and strategy and get into proper consulting? You've also been meaning to diversify your revenue streams with digital products. You want to optimize for freedom, fascination, and financial upside.

These four distinct phases of the freelance journey bring to my mind's eye the faces of people I've coached, consoled, and cajoled—smart, interesting, capable freelancers like Nate the new virtual assistant, Robert the grizzled business consultant, and Jen the translator-turned-copywriter.

NINE COUNTERINTUITIVE MOVES
FOR LIFE-CHANGING FREELANCE INCOME

Nine out of ten freelancers I chat with mention higher income obliquely, but find it difficult to come right out and say: "I want more money."

Why is that?

Many of us are taught explicitly or through household and cultural osmosis that money is dangerous or morally suspect. Decent people shouldn't want more of it. Certainly, creative people should, like epiphytes in the jungle, subsist on an airy diet of peace, love, and art.

Figuring out what to charge is hard because our subconscious beliefs about money can sabotage us once we have businesses. We don't learn about pricing in school, creative projects don't have set prices, and the best pricing advice can seem counterintuitive. Meanwhile, creative projects blur the line between play and labor.

How should we feel about asking people to pay a premium for enjoyable work that comes easily to us?

By the time we reach adulthood we've got mental backpacks filled with heavy souvenirs—stories and beliefs, ideas we've plucked from books or absorbed through conversation, and painful mistakes and mental hang-ups that constrain our thoughts and actions.

The same way it's impossible to run at full speed with sixty pounds on your back, it's impossible to face the prospect of earning *great* money as a freelancer with a thrilling lightness and eager expectation until you discard the beliefs, false assumptions, and bad habits that weigh you down.

The process of examining our relationship with money and upgrading our beliefs about it is gradual, not fast, and winding, not linear. This reflection necessarily happens while our lives unfold, our financial needs evolve, and our traitorous hearts pepper us with hard-to-answer questions: What do I want to do? What do I want? What's the money even for?

Freelancers want many things, ranging from honorable commitments to providing for one's family to all sorts of fantastical bucket-list items: Pay off school loans. Take your grandmother to visit her sister in Japan. Take your husband to watch his fill of live rugby matches in New Zealand. Adopt. Do a project for an iconic brand like Patagonia. Start a brewery.

When work gets tangled up with our identity and beliefs, and prices get tangled up with our histories and dreams, an invoice for a long-form case study or vampire cat illustration takes on lush significance: What am I doing with my life? Why am I freelancing? Why are we out of the good mustard?

No wonder pricing is a hard, crusty knot!

Most of us get into freelancing not because we're obsessed with money, but because we want time affluence. This desire for control over our time is so common among entrepreneurs that I started collecting quotes:

- Venture capitalist Naval Ravikant sums it up this way: "The ultimate purpose of money is so you do not have to be in a specific place at a specific time doing anything you don't want to do."

NINE COUNTERINTUITIVE MOVES
FOR LIFE-CHANGING FREELANCE INCOME

- Jason Fried, founder of Basecamp and Hey, said: "This is not about getting rich (though there's certainly nothing wrong with that). Instead, for me, making money is about freedom. When you owe people money, they own you—or, at least, they own your schedule. As long as you remain profitable, the timeline is yours to create."

- Author and book marketing expert Tim Grahl expresses a similar idea in even simpler terms: "I wanted to live a life where nobody could make a claim on my time without my approval."

Freelancing is a career path, business model, and lifestyle all at once, and it's quite possible, even probable, to make life-changing money.

Just don't expect it to be easy. Anyone who tells you freelancing is easy is stupid, lying, or trying to sell you something. Freelancing qualifies as Type II fun, which hunter and conservationist Steven Rinella once described this way:

The lowest, cheapest grade of fun is things that are actually fun while you're doing it. The highest grade of fun is things that are miserable while you're doing it, but they're fun to remember. And that kind of fun is more valuable. So like a rollercoaster is very low grade, not important fun. Suffering is a high grade, important fun. Because later when you're sitting around being like, "That sucked! It was so much fun!" No one ever like, five years down the road goes like, "Remember that rollercoaster? Woo-hoo! That was a good time.[1]

Though freelancing has more in common with stalking a Dall ram in the Alaskan wilderness than a trip to the grocery store, we can make specific choices that make freelancing a tad bit easier over time. Setting smart, strategic prices is one of them.

This book is for growth-minded freelancers who want to make more money, and it will help you regardless of where you are on the freelance journey: Moonlighter, Hustler, Lifestyler, or Diversifier.

In part one, we'll proceed straight to the practical steps for identifying the seven numbers you must know to set smart, strategic prices.

Part two kicks off with some wayfinding. Knowing where you want to be in three years will help you set your next three priorities for the near future and stay focused.

I'll ask you to make the unconscious conscious by putting your beliefs about money on the table and determining whether they're serving you and could possibly use an upgrade.

Many freelancers—especially creatives—need to believe in their worthiness before they can start charging what they're worth. To that end, I'll examine five limiting beliefs about money and explain what artists and creative entrepreneurs have in common and what they don't. Money is an emotionally charged subject for most people, freelancers included, and yet it's a tool, too, one that we need to pay bills and can use to bankroll freedom and do more good in the world.

Next, I'll ask you to take your vitamins. Vitamins are the crucial lessons, principles, and best practices that complement

NINE COUNTERINTUITIVE MOVES
FOR LIFE-CHANGING FREELANCE INCOME

the pricing process. Having smart, strategic prices is one thing; actually winning projects at those prices is another. This chapter will fortify you with some of my best thinking and advice for navigating various real-world situations. Following the right principles can mean earning thousands more.

Finally, I answer the questions about pricing I get asked most often and provide a condensed version of the pricing process. You'll revisit your prices many times over the course of your freelance career, and if you don't want to re-read this whole book, you can skip straight to the last chapter and run a victory lap.

Some freelancers will change their minds, change their prices, and change their lives. Why shouldn't you be one of them? Why not step out and up into a bigger vision for your work, creativity, and life? Why not give yourself permission to get a little goofy with excitement imagining your imminent transformation?

There's never been a better time to move upstream. You can be one of the hands-on creatives or problem-solving consultants who genuinely serves your clients while also not leaving money on the table.

This life-changing surplus is available right now to freelancers with the confidence to reach for what I call "free money." There are millions of value-conscious clients out there eager to hire someone with your skill set and happy to pay a premium for the right outcomes and a better overall experience.

Ample opportunity exists, and some creative entrepreneur is going to connect with those clients. Why not you? The extra money you could be charging is sitting right there. Why not reach out and take it?

This book is your clarifying, confidence-boosting map to what free money symbolizes for you. What is the extra money for? What would become possible? Take a moment to picture it. Breathe in. Smile.

This is the start of something new, and it's going to be good, Type II fun. Grab your journal and a pen, and let's get to work.

PART I:

Pricing

"Charge whatever will make you excited to do the work."

—Jay Clouse

MOVE ONE:

Find Your Survival Number

WHEN I WAS GROWING UP, MY FAMILY PLAYED MONOPOLY WITH A SPECIAL RULE THAT MADE IT MORE EXCITING AND UNPREDICTABLE, AND EASIER FOR THE KIDS TO WIN, TOO.

One of us would pay to get out of jail or pay a penalty after drawing a Chance or Community Chest card, and that money went into the kitty in the middle of the board. Whoever landed on Free Parking next got the stack of colorful bills.

With one roll of the dice, a player on the brink of bankruptcy could suddenly be flush with cash: "I'm back in it, baby!" This always elicited a groan from the other players who had nearly forced the lucky dog out of the game.

Freelancing is a game with its own surprising twists and unexpected endings, but unlike Monopoly, it pays in real cash and many people can win at the same time.

Freelancing is a positive-sum game.

If you're not winning at freelancing right now, invent a new game you can win. The wins you're after aren't big paydays but incremental gains and percentage increases. Tiny moves stack up over time and represent thousands in extra income.

Take my coaching client Kellie, for example. Once she realized she was undercharging, she summoned her courage and emailed her client. She told them she needed to raise her prices. Here's what happened next:

I just got a $500 per month raise. I usually write about four blog posts for them each month, and that was the deliverable I knew I was undercharging for. But, I look at the even bigger picture. They were my number three client last year in terms of billables. So, this represents a big difference when you look at it that way. It's also a huge confidence boost for me. THANK YOU!

What follows is the same step-by-step process Kellie followed as she was setting new rates and changing the game for herself. You're going to pinpoint seven crucial numbers that will help you do the same:

- Survival Number
- True Availability
- Survival Rate
- Dream Number
- Dream Rate
- Pessimistic Price
- Weirdly Precise

NINE COUNTERINTUITIVE MOVES
FOR LIFE-CHANGING FREELANCE INCOME

You're also going to answer questions that seem basic and boring at first glance, but your answers will dictate what a satisfying freelance lifestyle looks like for you:

- How many weeks of vacation do you want to take over the next year?
- What's a good ballpark number of holidays, sick days, and personal days?
- Is your freelance goal to make extra money on the side or to do it full-time?
- What was your after-tax salary or annual income at your last full-time job?
- What minimum amount must you earn each month to not go into debt?
- How much does running your business cost each month?
- What percentage of gross revenue goes to local, state, and federal taxes?
- How many hours do you work during a typical week?
- How many of those hours do you spend on client projects?

In "Hunted Down," a detective story by Charles Dickens, the protagonist observes, "A very little key will open a very heavy door."[1] Smart pricing is your very little key. The wrong rates keep you locked inside disappointment, discouragement, and disillusionment. The right rates bring in your target, life-changing income. They boost your confidence. They bankroll your desired lifestyle.

Step One: Find Your Survival Number

My friend Nick True at Mapped Out Money gives this advice: Widen the gap. Whether you earned $1,000, $10,000, or $100,000 freelancing last year, the only way to get ahead financially is to widen the gap between your spending and earning. Either you consistently earn more than you spend, or the opposite. It's common cents (sorry, I had to).

So, take this opportunity to run your numbers and figure out what minimum monthly income you need, even if you're one of those glorious individuals who doesn't struggle in the slightest to live within your means.

Estimate Your Average Monthly Personal Expenses

This is the easiest way to estimate your monthly personal expenses:

1. Export bank and credit card statements for the last three months.
2. Add up ninety days' worth of transactions.
3. Divide that total by three to get your up-to-date monthly average for personal expenses.

You may be tempted to cull "unusual" expenses. However, I recommend keeping all the expenses in your total except for huge, once-in-seven-years expenses, such as a down payment on a house or the $10,000 you spent on a Siberian tiger in Vegas (best night of your life).

There is no such thing as a "normal" month of spending. A new timing belt in your truck, antibiotics for that gnarly cat bite, the *luchador* mask you wanted for Halloween—unforeseen bills and purchases always come up. Count on it. "Budget" is just another word for plan, and a sensible monthly spending plan will always include padding in the form of a "Stuff I Didn't Plan For" line item.

Open Business Checking and Savings Accounts Yesterday

Some freelancers have one checking account that resembles a kitchen junk drawer with rubber bands, batteries, and mysterious spare keys jumbled together.

This messy approach creates confusion and friction. You don't really know how much money you have. You don't have visibility and end up spending money that you should have earmarked for taxes, not a makeover and photo shoot.

You have two practical ways to remedy the situation:

1. Open dedicated business checking and savings accounts. With business expenses separate from personal, accounting will be much easier. You can likely get free or

low-cost accounts from an online business bank or local credit union.

2. Read *Profit First* by Mike Michalowicz. Much overspending traces back to a lack of visibility. Mike's metaphorical envelope system for managing cash flow makes it easier to see how much cash you really have available.

Since I started using the *Profit First* system, I've avoided accidentally overpaying myself and have gotten a tax refund every year. That's much more enjoyable than gutting my business savings account each April and giving Uncle Sam "extra" money I thought was mine to keep.

All right, Business Dad moment over.

Add Up Your Business-Related Spending

Every freelance business has expenses and potential tax write-offs. To figure out your cost of doing business for an average month, follow the same process as above with your business account and credit card statements.

Those of you who already have dedicated business checking and savings accounts can follow these steps:

- Add up ninety days' worth of transactions.
- Divide the total by three to get your up-to-date monthly average for business expenses.

Those of you who don't have dedicated business checking and savings accounts will need to revisit your personal statements (ideally, exported as a .csv file):

- Either make a copy of the file and delete all the personal expenses, leaving only business expenses, or create a new spreadsheet using the list of business expenses below. Then copy and paste the business stuff mixed in with personal expenses.

- Once you've got the rough monthly total, add an extra line item for 10 percent. That "Stuff I Didn't Plan For" padding will cover irregular expenses, such as domain registrations.

Incomplete List of Business Expenses

- Administrative / office supplies (e.g., postage, printing, paper)
- Office space / overhead
- Internet service
- Phone / mobile service
- Tools (e.g., laptop)
- Software and subscriptions (e.g., email, web hosting, cloud storage, accounting software, time tracking, project management)
- Memberships (e.g., associations, industry groups)
- Local licenses and taxes

- Marketing

- Meals and entertainment (e.g., coffee with clients)

- Business travel / conferences

- Education and professional development (e.g., books, business coaching)

- Professional services (e.g., bookkeeping, tax prep, attorney fees, designer)

Figure Out Your Tax Percentage

Once you've got a firm grip on your personal and business expenses, it's time to think about everyone's favorite party topic: taxes. (Or is it death?)

The number we're after is the percentage of your gross freelance revenue you paid in taxes last year.

Each freelancer's percentage goes up or down based on lots of factors: your city, county, state, and country; your gross revenue, tax write-offs, and any tax credits and deductions; investments, assets, and other sources of income; and your legal entity structure, filing status, and overall tax strategy.

At the time of writing, Austria had a tax rate of 55 percent, the highest in the world. Bermuda, Monaco, the Bahamas, Andorra, and the United Arab Emirates (UAE) had no income tax.

Is your head hurting yet? Excellent. That means the real work has begun.

NINE COUNTERINTUITIVE MOVES
FOR LIFE-CHANGING FREELANCE INCOME

To find your tax percentage, you have three options, with the first being the most reliable:

1. Look at your last tax return. (Or ask your accountant to tell you.)
2. Ask two local freelancers with comparable income what their tax rate was, add their numbers, and divide by two to get your ballpark number.
3. Make a conservative guess, such as 25 or 30 percent of your gross income.

If you choose option one, here are the steps for freelancers paying US taxes:

- Find your total income, usually on Line 9 of Form 1040. (For the one reader who cares, the total income number in your tax return will be close to the net income your accounting software shows for the year.)
- Find your total tax, usually on Line 24 of Form 1040.
- Multiply your total tax by 100, then divide that number by your total income.

For example, let's say your total income was $50,000, and your total tax was $9,000. $9,000 × 100 / $50,000 = 18.

Eighteen percent is your effective tax percentage.

Yes, this percentage can change from year to year, but it's a good enough rule of thumb for our purposes here.

If you don't live in the United States, run searches online until you find the right set of steps for your country. Better yet, hire a tax professional. (As I mentioned in the disclaimer on the copyright page, I am not one, and therefore don't know all the rules and nuances.)

No matter where you are at, don't get bogged down with this step. Pinpoint an approximate tax percentage and charge ahead (pun intended).

Calculate Your Survival Number

You brave readers who have persisted this far now have three important numbers: your monthly personal expenses, business expenses, and tax percentage.

In five steps you will grab your Survival Number by the scruff of its skinny neck. Your Survival Number is the minimum you need to earn during a twelve-month period.

Here are the steps to calculate it:

1. Subtract your tax percentage from 100. If your tax rate is 20 percent, then: 100 - 20 = 80. We'll call that 80 percent your After-Tax Revenue Percentage, which was also the name of my first puppy.

2. Add up your personal and business expenses. This total represents the monthly "nut" you need to cover all bills. Let's say your personal expenses and business expenses add up to $3,000 a month.

NINE COUNTERINTUITIVE MOVES
FOR LIFE-CHANGING FREELANCE INCOME

3. Multiply that number ($3,000) by 100: $3,000 ×100 = $300,000.

4. Divide that number by your After-Tax Revenue Percentage (80 percent). $300,000 / 80 = $3,750. That's your monthly revenue target. You must earn $3,750 each month to cover your $3,000 monthly nut, set aside $750 for taxes, and essentially break even.

5. Calculate your yearly Survival Number. $3,750 per month ×12 months = $45,000. You must make at least that much to avoid getting yourself into debt and financial trouble.

Note: If you live in a two-income household, take your share of monthly personal expenses as a dollar amount, add in your business expenses and taxes, and use it to calculate your Survival Number, and later, your Survival Rate.

You now have your Survival Number. You have successfully completed the first grueling stage of the *Free Money* math gauntlet. Congratulations.

Remember:

- If you're not winning at freelancing right now, invent a game you can win by setting new rates.

- The right rates will boost your confidence and bring in your target, life-changing income.

- The first number you need is your realistic minimum monthly income.

- Once you add in your business expenses and estimated taxes, you'll have your Survival Number, or what you need to earn in twelve months to not go into debt.
- Later, you'll use that number to figure out your Survival Rate.

See you in Move Two, where we'll estimate your True Availability for client work.

MOVE TWO:

◇◇◇◇◇◇◇◇◇◇

Find Your True Availability

ON A THURSDAY IN NOVEMBER 2021, MY FRIEND TIM RHYNE MET UP WITH SEVERAL CYCLISTS OUTSIDE OF DENVER, COLORADO, TO GO FOR A RIDE. An hour later, the group came out of tree coverage and into a canyon, and a wild, powerful gust of wind shoved Tim from the inside of the lane to the outside.

As Tim struggled to regain control, his bike fishtailed. He crashed and hit the pavement with so much force that he shattered his collarbone, broke three ribs, and partially collapsed one of his lungs. Tim's momentum carried him across the asphalt, which caused severe abrasions on his shoulders and back.

When he came to his senses, Tim realized he was lucky to be alive. A hospital stay, surgery, and weeks of physical therapy followed. Tim's work took a back seat while he recovered from his injuries.

Now, let's flash back to several months earlier in 2021, when I had helped Tim overhaul his design studio's fee structure. Soon after, Tim won multiple large projects. The studio had cash reserves for the first time. Thanks to that surplus, Tim didn't have to return to work right away. He was able to focus on recovering from his injuries.

Step Two: Figure Out Your Available Work Weeks

You're in the middle of the same process Tim and I followed, and you're going to avoid two mistakes that freelancers often make when setting their prices:

1. Overestimating how many hours they can work in a given month
2. Failing to differentiate between billable and non-billable hours

Those two mistakes may seem benign, but they produce oversimplified math like this, which sets you up for frustration and failure:

- 4 weeks × 40-hour work week = 160 hours per month
- $5,000 per month / 160 = $31.25 per hour

This math, and the plan it implies, would require you not just to work but to bill 160 or more hours every month.

That simply won't happen, as too many variables can and will change. The only thing we can count on as freelancers is things not going according to plan. A single client email or gust of wind can wreck your plans and that month's earning.

The better approach to figuring out how much time you can realistically spend on client projects is starting not with hours in a month but with your "available" work weeks in a year.

That way, your pricing will account for natural and inevitable fluctuations in productivity, billing, and earning from one month to the next. Fatter months can cover the leaner ones. Busy months can fund vacations and absences.

Lots of us plan to slow down, at least a little, during the holidays. If, like me, you anticipate losing half of December to travel, ugly Christmas sweater parties, or a delicious few days away from the old inbox, then you'll need to over-earn in the preceding months and pay December's bills with "old" income.

Here are the three steps for figuring out your available work weeks:

1. Add up the days in the next twelve months you won't work.

Count vacations (e.g., spring break with the kids), national holidays, potential sick days, and other time off. Don't count weekends. Some freelancers tell themselves they need to work seven days a week, but that's neither true nor sustainable—even if you are in the startup phase. Don't risk burning out before you've truly begun.

A typical year for me includes three or four weeks of vacation, quarterly offsite planning days, a business retreat, a couple of conferences that monopolize two workdays, and celebrating various holidays, including Thanksgiving and Christmas.

My three kids are school age, and I enjoy going on their field trips to the zoo, pumpkin patch, museums, you get the idea. I call this "Field Trip Freedom," and it's one of the weird metrics I use to measure my success as a freelancer. Knowing that I will put in only one or two hours of meaningful work on field trip days, I treat these days as a wash and tack on another five "personal days" to the total number I plan to miss.

So, across an entire year, I won't work around forty days. What's your number?

2. Divide the number of days you won't work by seven and round up.

We can't plan for every eventuality, so I'd encourage you to not get tangled up with too much precision here. Certain days and weeks you won't work much, if at all. For me, after I divide forty by seven, that number ends up being around six weeks.

How many weeks will you be "out of office"?

3. Subtract the out-of-office number from fifty-two to get available work weeks.

Once you have your number of weeks, take a mental step back and give it an appraising look. Are you being realistic? And are you imagining the life you really want for yourself? You may need to subtract one or two more weeks to be on the safe and generous side.

Here's what my scenario looks like:

52 weeks − 6 weeks off = 46 available work weeks

For the sake of simplicity, we'll say that's a realistic number for you, too, and use that number for the rest of the exercises and calculations.

Add Up Your Available Work Hours

Now that you've got your available weeks, let's figure out the number of hours you will work in an average week. For our purposes, I define "work" as income-producing activities, along with the many other tasks and projects required to sustain my business.

My workday starts around 9:00 a.m. and runs to 5:30 p.m. Lunch takes thirty minutes, or an hour-and-a-half if I'm driving to meet someone. My work week ends Friday at lunch, though I usually spend Friday afternoons on what I call "Friday Zero," a weekly windup ritual that includes "Inbox Zero," "Desktop Zero," and "Downloads Folder Zero."

My weekend rule isn't strictly "No Work," rather "No Client Work." If I want to put in the occasional ninety-minute block on Saturday mornings because I want to write, research, or play with a new idea, that's up to me.

All told, my availability averages out to thirty-eight hours per week.

These questions will help you determine your available work hours in an average week:

- When do you usually start and stop working?
- How long do you take for lunch?

- Do you work on weekends? How much? Do you really want to work on Saturday and Sunday, or do you tell yourself you have to?

- How many hours do you work during a typical week?

- Is your current pace healthy, sustainable, and enjoyable?

That last question may deserve deep reflection. In the United States we've created a wacky cult of thought and practice around optimization, efficiency, and a misshapen gray balloon with the word "success" written on it. (We'll deflate that balloon later in this book.)

Each of us must dance along the boundary between what's possible and beneficial. As the sworn enemy of busyness and burnout, I don't advocate for more hours and longer days. Hustle culture delivers on all the wrong promises. No one wins the race to burnout. I encourage you to opt out.

Work that feels like play is one of the most satisfying gifts we have, and work that feels like toil is one of the heaviest burdens we carry.

So, as you think through how many hours you'll work in an average week, don't set your sights on the maximum, but on a healthy, sustainable number. What's the point of the extra money if you're too busy to enjoy it?

That "no free time" trap was the one a coaching client named Amanda had fallen into: "I'm happy with my business revenue, but I'm way too busy. [. . .] I was so busy that I didn't have time to enjoy it."

What's your number? Pick one that holds this beautiful, yet razor-edged thing called work in healthy tension with other pursuits and commitments that you value as much or more.

Did I get a little preachy there? I thought so. Yes, I enjoyed it, too.

Step Three: Calculate Available Time Inventory

Now that you know your work weeks in a year and a healthy number of weekly work hours, you can calculate your approximate time inventory for the entire year.

- Multiply work weeks by hours per week.
- Give yourself a lingering hug.

Here's what I get when I multiply my available work weeks and average work hours: 46 × 38 = 1,748 hours.

That's my available time inventory in a year. What's yours?

Step Four: Account for Effectiveness

Some of your available time inventory goes to billable work, but not all of it. Email and client communication will eat up time. You'll quote projects and put together proposals. You'll book an extra call to keep a project moving forward. You'll go for a walk to clear your head.

Non-billable tasks are termites that eat away at your money-making time. Unlike termites, some of these tasks provide essential structure and support to the business.

You must account for your business's administrative and operational needs in your pricing calculations, and you do that by estimating your "effectiveness." Effectiveness is the realistic percentage of total hours that you can spend on income-generating tasks and projects during a typical work week.

Building effectiveness into your rates will leave you with less anxiety about non-billable hours. As long as you hit a certain income target each month, you can afford to work less. Your prices will support your lifestyle, not the other way around.

Prices with effectiveness built in will give you the cushion to absorb more of life's punches. In the summer of 2022, I brought a souvenir home from a trip to Mexico: giardiasis. The parasite negatively affected my productivity for over a month, but I was still able to pay my family's bills.

Here are the steps for finding your effectiveness:

- Estimate the percentage of hours you can effectively bill each week.
- Turn your percentage (e.g., 60 percent) into a decimal (e.g., 0.60).
- Multiply your available time inventory by the decimal.

Here are my numbers:

NINE COUNTERINTUITIVE MOVES
FOR LIFE-CHANGING FREELANCE INCOME

- 60 percent of my available hours spent on billable work is realistic for me.

- 1,748 work hours per year × 0.60 effectiveness = 1,048 billable hours.

- 1,048 hours is how much time I'll have each year for billable work.

How many hours can you realistically bill in a year?

Let it be known that all this estimating is what former US president Dwight D. Eisenhower would call peace-time planning: "Peace-time plans are of no particular value, but peace-time planning is indispensable."

Your available work weeks, work hours, time inventory, and effectiveness will always be in flux. Some weeks you'll spend more time on billable projects, and other weeks, less. Tons of factors make our effectiveness go up or down, including the number of projects you juggle, children and other family obligations, the time of year, travel, health, emergencies, and countless other surprises we'll put in the "Life Happens" bucket.

Sudden illness changes your output, or a last-minute opportunity with a dream client motivates you to work (happily) through the weekend.

With that in mind, lean toward a more conservative effectiveness percentage and number of billable hours and move to the next chapter.

Remember:

- Freelancers overestimate how many hours we can work in a month.

- We work a lot of hours we can't directly bill to clients.

- Variables we can't predict or control affect how much work we do each week.

- A better approach to your pricing starts with the number of weeks you can realistically work in a year.

- From there, you can quickly estimate the average number of hours you work per week, your available time inventory, and your effectiveness.

- With those numbers in hand, you can figure out how many hours you can expect to bill in a year and base your smart, sustainable rates on that number.

See you in Move Three, where we'll find your Survival Rate and Dream Number.

MOVE THREE:

Find Your Survival Rate, Dream Number, and Dream Rate

A FRIDAY IN DECEMBER 2022 FOUND ME DRIVING DOWN TO UNADILLA, GEORGIA. If you're wondering what brings people to this tiny town, the answer is not much, other than pecan trees, Dooly State Prison, and the mayor, Myron Mixon, who also happens to be "the winningest man in barbecue."

Mixon earned the title by taking home more Grand Champion titles than anyone else in history. After my friend Joe made the pilgrimage down to Myron Mixon's BBQ Cooking School and told me about the experience, I thought, "I want to do that someday."

Only a peculiar individual would be eager to pay $900, drive 350 miles (560 kilometers for you metric lovers), and spend an entire weekend freezing his derriere while watching a stranger prepare a whole hog and other meats for the smoker. If I have no plans to open a restaurant, own a food truck, or start a catering company, why would I make that kind of investment in upping my barbeque game? Because I wanted to.

Will Rogers might have been addressing a room full of freelancers when he said, "The goal isn't more money. The goal is living life on your terms."

Isn't having the freedom and flexibility to spend "work hours" on other projects, passions, and people the point of building an independent career?

We've all got friends and family motivated by the sense of security or predictability that full-time employment offers, but chances are, you've chosen the freelance path because you want your calendar to look a certain way. You want your days to have plenty of space for pickleball or *shibori*, extreme ironing or romance novels, greyhound rescue or volunteering at your kid's school.

Now that you've found your Survival Number and True Availability for client work, you're only a hop, skip, and a jump away from prices that do for your lifestyle what smoked brisket does for my belly. Let's find your Survival Rate.

Step Five: Find Your Survival Rate

Your Survival Rate is the minimum you must make per billable hour to cover time you can't or won't bill for, and still hit your Survival Number for the year.

Notice I used the word "make," not "charge." When you're able to charge more than you need to make to survive, you start a virtuous cycle:

- You over-earn.

NINE COUNTERINTUITIVE MOVES
FOR LIFE-CHANGING FREELANCE INCOME

- You pay your bills early.
- The leftovers become savings.
- You stop living month to month.
- You pay your monthly "salary" with old income.
- You start chipping away at long-term financial goals.
- You take true holidays instead of peeking at email.

That tantalizing future hinges on what you charge in the present. To build a sustainable freelance business, you cannot make less than your Survival Rate. Otherwise, you risk coming up short and going into debt.

Plug your numbers from the previous exercises into this Survival Rate calculation:

Annual Survival Number / Annual Billable Hours = Survival Rate

My family of five living in Knoxville, Tennessee, needs $9,000 each month, or $108,000 a year. That $108,000 is my Survival Number. Based on my calculations, I will work 1,748 work hours in twelve months, but I can realistically bill only about 60 percent of that: 1,048 hours.

My Survival Rate calculation looks like this:

$108,000 / 1,048 billable hours = $103.05 an hour

My Survival Rate is $103.

Whether I charge by the hour or by the project, I need to make at least $103 per hour for 1,048 hours over a twelve-month period.

Based on the cost of living in your city, my Survival Rate of $103 may seem ridiculously high, alarmingly low, or just right. For example, if you live in Cebu City, Philippines, your Survival Rate can be much lower than mine. Based on my research online at the time of writing, a single freelancer could get by on $1,000 per month in this metropolis with a tropical climate and easy access to beaches, and diving locations.[1] A one-bedroom apartment in a central location might set you back $300, and you'd need another $600 for monthly living costs.

Contrast Cebu City with New York City, where studio and one-bedroom apartments start around $2,000 before going to the moon.

Your location, lifestyle, and other variables, including other people you support financially, affect what you must make and therefore charge. You can't blindly copy the freelancer who lives down the road or across the world because that person may have vastly different immediate needs and long-term goals.

When I first started freelancing, I could get by on $1,100 in Knoxville. These days, that wouldn't even cover my family's housing costs, let alone health care and the monthly mound of chicken nuggets for three ravenous, picky children.

So, strip away any vanity or value judgments for now and dig down to the real math at the bottom of your financial needs.

What is your Survival Rate?

Step Six: Find Your Dream Number

Once you've calculated your Survival Rate, you know what you must make per billable hour to support your current lifestyle.

Our next objective is thinking beyond mere survival. Most of us aren't satisfied with our lives when our time and money is spread thinner than mustard on a gas-station sandwich. No one gets into freelancing to simply break even.

Though most freelancers don't talk openly about their income goals, and some won't admit the real number to themselves, most freelancers I've spoken with want significantly more money. The best things in life may be free, but everything else requires cash.

This next exercise requires a heavy helping of honesty: What, specifically, would you do with extra income? How much would you like to make really?

Set a timer for fifteen minutes.

Write down a *meaningful amount of money per month* for any of the categories below relevant to you:

- Debt paydown (e.g., credit cards, student loans, car loan, mortgage)

- Short-term saving (e.g., emergency fund, upcoming travel, holiday gifts)

- Long-term saving (e.g., car, down payment, wedding)

- Investing (e.g., retirement, real estate, stock, crypto)

- Lifestyle goals (e.g., vacation home, RV, private school for kids)

- Giving (e.g., faith community, nonprofits, causes, friends, family)

- Bucket list (e.g., restoring a vintage Airstream, extended vacation in Japan)

- Passion projects (e.g., recording an album, learning Spanish)

Over the years my coaching clients have shared a beautiful diversity of dreams and goals with me. May this small sample inspire you:

- Move to a new city.
- Buy clothes you really love.
- Become a digital nomad.
- Take horseback riding lessons.
- Pay other people's medical bills.
- Start a furniture flipping side hustle.
- Go to Norway to enjoy the architecture.
- Buy original art without worrying about prices.
- Help nieces and nephews with college tuition.
- Pursue singing and scientific research . . . at the same time.

NINE COUNTERINTUITIVE MOVES
FOR LIFE-CHANGING FREELANCE INCOME

- Hand out wads of cash to cashiers and servers around Christmas time.
- Create a fund of some sort for kids needing help with their artistic endeavors.

Don't worry about creating a comprehensive list. All you're after right now is a ballpark number to help you do this calculation:

- Add up the numbers above. How much extra do you want each month to make progress on these financial and lifestyle goals?
- Multiply that number by twelve.
- Add that annualized total to your Survival Number. That's your Dream Number.

Knowing your Dream Number is a fork in a path. To the right is a wide, well-trodden trail of complacency, resignation, and fake contentment that says, "So many people are worse off. I should just be satisfied with what I have." (Contentment is an admirable trait, but are you content? Be honest.)

To the left you see a narrower, steeper, riskier trail. If you really let yourself dream, what's up the path and around the next bend?

Note: If you struggled to pick categories and estimate monthly amounts, just multiply your Survival Number by 1.5. That 50 percent bump will enable you to save more, extend your financial runway, and exercise your walkaway power, meaning reject boring, tedious, or low-paying projects because you don't need the money. After you reach that 1.5 goal, you can set a new one.

Example: My Freelance Dream Number

For me to move past surviving to truly thriving would mean I was making definitive progress each month on these specific, near-term goals:

- Emergency fund that covers at least six months' worth of my family's Survival Number.
- Nice basement and pool for hosting and hanging out. We want to have the house where our kids and their friends want to hang during their teenage years. That way, we can spend more time with our kids during their adolescent years and keep closer tabs on all their hooligan friends, too. Yep, we're those parents.
- Writing cabin in the backyard.

To do that, I'd need to make an extra $3,750 per month, or $45,000 per year.

My Dream Number calculation goes like this:

$108,000 (Survival Number) + $45,000 = $153,000 (Dream Number).

What's yours?

Step Seven: Find Your Dream Rate

Now it's time to give your rates a pep talk. Your Dream Rate is what you must make per billable hour to hit your Dream Number. That Dream Rate encompasses your immediate personal needs, business expenses, taxes, time away from work, non-billable work time, and meaningful progress on your long-term financial goals.

To turn your Dream Number into your Dream Rate, you'll use the same easy math that produced your Survival Rate:

Annual Dream Number / Billable Hours = Dream Rate

Example: My Freelance Dream Rate

I'm going to calculate my Dream Rate in a moment, but first, I'll show again all the steps we've taken thus far:

- 52 weeks a year – 6 weeks not working = 46 work weeks.

- 46 work weeks per year × 38 average work hours per week = 1,748 work hours per year.

- 1,748 work hours × 0.60 (or, 60 percent effectiveness) = 1,048 billable hours.

- My Survival Number of $108,000 per year (or, $9,000 per month) / 1,048 billable hours = a Survival Rate of $103 per hour.

- A Dream Number averaged out to $3,750 extra per month, or $12,750 total per month, or $153,000 per year.

- My Dream Number ($153,000) / 1,048 billable hours = a Dream Rate of $146 per hour.

As I mentioned earlier, your cost of living may be much lower or higher than mine. We're in different places, literally and figuratively. Your lifestyle goals may surpass mine by a huge, I-want-to-buy-a-retreat-center-in-Hawaii margin. That's to be expected. What you're after is simple math and sturdy rates on which you can build a thriving freelance business.

How Does Your Dream Rate Make You Feel?

Before we move to the next step, I want you to reflect on how you feel right now.

When I first hacked together the steps in this process in 2015 and laid eyes on my Dream Rate, my excitement at being practical and discovering what I really needed to be making curdled into discouragement.

Sure, I was reconnecting with my dreams of getting out of debt and buying a beach house. But those dreams seemed like the peaks of impossibly remote mountains on the northern border of Ridiculous. Make that much per billable hour? Yeah, right. I could as easily sprout wings and fly to the summit of Everest.

My wife and I were broke, and with our growing family and the cost of living in Knoxville, my business would need to consistently bring in twice as much. Not a little more, but double. I didn't see how we were going to get there.

Did being honest about my dreams solve all our problems instantly? Of course not. But that real, raw insight did jar me out of complacency. The surest way to miss a goal is to keep it hidden from yourself. You increase your odds of success by facing the truth in all its uncomfortable detail. Hard math told me I wasn't making enough to burn down our trash heap of credit card debt.

NINE COUNTERINTUITIVE MOVES
FOR LIFE-CHANGING FREELANCE INCOME

A burst of resolve followed the discouragement. I couldn't soar up to my Dream Number tomorrow, but I could do something, such as raise my prices by 10–15 percent.

My Dream Rate pointed at being debt free again.

Now, back to you: How does your Dream Rate make you feel? And what does it represent?

As your imagination comes out of hibernation and shakes itself like a groggy, scrawny bear, your goals will come into sharper focus. High-definition goals enable us to notice more opportunities and more strategies for achieving them. In *Be Your Future Self Now*, psychologist and author Dr. Benjamin Hardy explains why this happens: "Once you are clear and committed," he writes, "everything will filter through your goal—what psychologists call selective attention. You see what you're looking for. You see what you care about. What you focus on expands."[2]

You've already begun building your selective attention by finding these five crucial numbers and acknowledging the strong emotions they stir up:

- Survival Number
- True Availability
- Survival Rate
- Dream Number
- Dream Rate

Building on that trustworthy foundation of math, you can set a Pessimistic Price and make it Weirdly Precise as a final touch.

Knowing what you *must* charge based on your seven numbers will give you more peace and more steel when you talk to new clients.

Remember:

- Your Survival Rate is the minimum you must make per billable hour to hit your Survival Number for the year.

- You can't blindly copy other freelancers because a unique mix of variables, including your location, lifestyle, and people you support financially, determines what you must make and therefore charge.

- Your Dream Number represents the extra money you'd like to make each month to make definitive progress on financial and lifestyle goals and move beyond surviving to truly thriving.

- Your Dream Rate, or what you must make per billable hour to hit that Dream Number, accounts for your immediate personal needs, business expenses, taxes, time away from work, non-billable work time, and meaningful progress on your long-term financial goals.

- Finally, don't be surprised if your Dream Rate makes like a family reunion and stirs up strong emotions. And don't be afraid to lock yourself in a bathroom with your journal and write them all down.

Now, it's time to turn your Dream Rate into a Pessimistic Price.

MOVE FOUR:

Set Your Pessimistic Price

NOW THAT YOU'VE GOT YOUR DREAM RATE, YOU'RE PROBABLY ITCHING TO RUN THE FINAL LAP AND SET NEW PRICES FOR THE VARIOUS PROJECTS YOU DO.

Take a quick trip to Hawaii with me first.

Imagine you have a friend who owns a pineapple farm. Kimi makes you an offer: You can harvest the pineapples, sell them, and keep all the profits if you will maintain the property.

The idea intrigues you. You could bow out of your boring nine-to-five job, complete with crappy salary and your smothering, micromanaging boss, Bill Lumbergh also known as Lameburger. You could finally start betting on yourself!

Once you crunch some numbers for making the farm sustainable, your interest turns into excitement. If you were to sell a hundred pineapples per week at the farmer's market, you could cover your living expenses and taxes, pay off your student loans, and even save for a down payment on a house.

You commit to a twelve-month trial—can't be worse than Lameburger's delusional performance reviews and pep talks—and the first two months validate your decision. You manage to sell all fifty pineapples at your first farmer's market appearance. You stumble upon fifty more mature pineapple plants in an overgrown corner of the farm. You plant fifty pineapple crowns.

The average of fifty pineapples sold per week grows to eighty, but six months in, you can't ignore the obvious. No matter how much you water and prune those plants, each will produce only one flower stalk and one fruit. The crowns you planted won't produce fruit for another eighteen months at least. Your maximum yield has plateaued.

Desperate times call for denser spreadsheets, so you crunch more numbers and reach three conclusions:

- You can raise your prices. However, if you go any higher than an extra $1.00 extra per pineapple, you'll lose customers. Your pineapples are among the best, but the tourists in their creased Hawaiian shirts aren't sensitive enough to subtle differences in prime ripeness, sweetness, and quality to pay a premium.

- You can resell other farmers' pineapples. However, the logistics of sourcing, buying, and transporting the extra pineapples would take time. You can't magically multiply your own time, and the per-pineapple profit you could squeeze out probably wouldn't justify the effort and fuel costs.

NINE COUNTERINTUITIVE MOVES
FOR LIFE-CHANGING FREELANCE INCOME

- You can grow and sell other types of produce. The trouble is, you'd encounter the same problems with logistics and profit margin. Instead of having an obvious niche (The Pineapple Lady), your stand would be another generic one selling a variety of fruits and veggies.

You call Kimi and explain your conundrum. Savvy entrepreneur that she is, Kimi reframes the problem. The inherent limitations of arable acreage, growing cycles, and your personal inventory of time are capping how much you can earn.

"How can you change how much a single pineapple is worth?" she asks. "Let's turn your 'Twenty Pineapples Problem' into a 'Two Hundred Pineapples Opportunity.' For example, if you find ways to repackage the pineapples, you can charge more for them."

Together, the two of you brainstorm some new possibilities:

- Team up with other vendors to offer fresh-fruit subscriptions to local families.

- Dry each week's leftover pineapples and sell locally grown "snacks."

- Buy leftover pineapples from other vendors and juice them.

- Offer same-day pineapple delivery to local restaurants.

- Paint pineapples and sell them as décor.

In case you didn't already make the connection with freelancing, I'll make it painfully, fruitfully clear. A pineapple farmer can't pull twenty pineapples out of thin air, and a freelancer can't manufacture more hours.

Freelance clients may ask to buy time: "What's your hourly rate?" or "Can I buy some of your time?" You may have billed hourly in the past. Yet, the hourly model penalizes your gains in skill, speed, and expertise. Work faster, and you make less. That's a losing proposition if I ever saw one.

To make life-changing income, start selling outcomes, not hours. Don't sell "copywriting services at $75 an hour." Instead, take Kimi's advice and change the packaging. Dice, dry, and juice your precious pineapples. Offer "narrative, long-form case studies meticulously researched, expertly crafted, and delivered in ten days or less." The final price varies based on the full scope of the client's needs, timeline, and the project's potential value.

We'll examine more nuances of pricing models and pricing strategy later in the book. Right now, you're going to turn your new Dream Rate into smart, sustainable prices you can put in front of a client tomorrow.

Pick a Project and List the Tasks

Think of a project you'd like to sell more of and list all the tasks involved.

Use these categories to jog your memory, and be sure to include sneaky time-suckers, such as calls, emails, and project management:

- Scheduling, project setup, and ongoing project management
- Client communication, including emails, meetings, and phone calls
- Research and other prep work
- Actual creative work and deliverables
- Presenting, capturing feedback, making changes
- Admin work (e.g., project wrap-up, file delivery, and invoicing)

Add Up and Round Up the Total Time Required

What you're after here is the most accurate estimate you can muster. How long do you typically need to deliver the project, beginning to end, with all the project management and client experience pizzazz that entails?

Writing a long-form, narrative case study for one of my clients might look like this:

- Send email with onboarding questionnaire: 0.25 hr.
- Do kickoff call: 1.0 hr.
- Schedule interviews: 0.25 hr.
- Set up project docs: 0.50 hr.

FREE MONEY

- Create outline and do initial research: 1.5 hrs.
- Conduct two 30-minute interviews: 1.00 hr.
- Have interviews transcribed: 0.25 hr.
- Write first draft: 4 hrs.
- Finalize first draft & send to client for review: 1.5 hrs.
- Work through client's feedback and revisions: 1 hr.
- Work through final edits and spell check: 0.75 hr.
- Send final draft to client: 0.25 hr.

Total: 12.25 hrs.

Rounded-up estimate: 13 hrs.

If you are new to freelancing or you feel for time tracking what I feel for celery (intense loathing), write down your best guess for each task in fifteen-minute increments.

Don't worry about making perfect predictions. Time estimates are always squishy until you carefully track several projects and standardize your process. For now, ballpark the total time for your project, and round up to the next number.

If you have tracked your time during previous projects, this step will be straightforward for you:

- Log into your time-tracking app.
- Generate a report for a similar project.
- Cross-reference it with the task list you just created.

- Retroactively add time for any tasks or categories you didn't track.

What is your rounded-up time estimate?

Multiply Total Time By Your Dream Rate

In Move Three my math produced a Dream Rate of $146 per hour. My first stab at a price for case study projects came to $1,898:

13 hours × $146 / hour = $1,898.

What's your initial price?

Add a Buffer to Get Your Pessimistic Price

Some clients take *forever* to respond, and their radio silences cause delays and kill momentum. Other clients will be overly picky, indecisive, or straight-up irritating. They will take your patience to the very brink.

You can count on the twenty-two-minute call to soothe an ego and the fifteen-minute "favor," but you can't always bill Mr. Can We Move That Comma for those thirty-seven minutes. So how do you account for that extra time, good humor, and oomph required to heave some projects across the finish line?

Build a 20 percent buffer into your price on the front end. Budget for human nature.

I call this Pessimistic Pricing. Projects always evolve. Scope always creeps. If your prices are too lean, you'll start to resent clients for asking for more of your time. Important as strong boundaries and clear expectations are around extra work and billing, minor scope creep isn't worth ruining the relationship over. Doing that fifteen-minute "favor" now and again can preserve a relationship that will one day represent $15,000 in lifetime value.

Expect clients to be on their worst behavior, not their best.

Benjamin Franklin might have been speaking to you and me when in 1736 he gave this advice to the people of Philadelphia worried about fires: "An ounce of prevention is worth a pound of cure."

When I add 20 percent to my $1,898 case study price, or rather multiply it by 1.2, I get a Pessimistic Price of $2,277.

What's your Pessimistic Price?

Gauge Your Enthusiasm

Once you have your Pessimistic Price, pepper it with questions:

- Would I be glad to make this amount of money for this amount of work?
- Is the price high enough to feel exciting, even a little risky?
- Does the price feel like a step forward for the business?

NINE COUNTERINTUITIVE MOVES
FOR LIFE-CHANGING FREELANCE INCOME

If the price doesn't hold up under scrutiny, ask yourself:

- Why do I have misgivings?
- Does the price feel high or low?
- Is the price or your confidence the real problem?
- What would need to be true for me to feel good about this price?

Adjust the price by small increments of $25 or $50 (or the equivalent in your local currency) until you've got a new price that feels better.

Now, imagine putting it in front of an existing client.

How do you think they will respond?

Most freelancers already have a complicated relationship with money, and with their prices by association, so speculating about people's responses can stir up strong feelings.

Graduating to higher project fees may force you to part ways with loyal clients, including family, friends, and early referrals. Maybe you feel guilty about leaving them behind. Maybe you feel like you're being greedy. Aren't you repaying their loyalty with a punch in the gut? These are the people who helped you grow your business! Maybe you should be content with what you already have. After all, so many people are worse off.

Step out of those emotional riptides for a moment and remember how you reached this point. You colored in the details about your immediate needs and long-term goals. You budgeted for human nature. Then, math did the rest.

You know what you must charge and why. Not to sound cold-blooded, but the clients and projects who got you here won't get you *there*, that mountain off in the distance. One day, next week or next year, you'll put your smart, strategic, sustainable price in front of a loyal client. They will balk. A person you care about will walk away, believing your new prices are "too high."

You'll have to let them because all your past clients can't or won't grow with you. Your metamorphosis may be messy, nonlinear, and whatever the opposite of "cheered on by my admiring friends, family, and clients" is.

Can you live with that? Yes, you can.

You will remind yourself that only your new prices can bankroll the lifestyle you really want. No matter what some clients may believe, those prices represent your common sense, not your lack of gratitude. They're a sign that you are thinking like both an entrepreneur and an artist now. You can be both, and you're no longer satisfied with trading time for money. You've found a better paradigm, and pricing to go with it.

Hope isn't a strategy, so you've had to become a better advocate for your needs and desires. You will risk some people's temporary displeasure with losing your underpriced services while you transform your business.

For example, one freelance developer named Jess got her start building websites for nonprofits. Eventually, she realized that her price-sensitive nonprofit clients couldn't stomach the $10,000 starting price she needed to charge. However, for fashion influencers, coffee roasters, or clean energy startups, the same price was quite reasonable.

Like Jess, you may discover that you need to pivot to a new niche where people won't balk at your prices. You need to form new relationships. Growing your network will take time and effort. The sooner you face this reality, the sooner you will start hitting your income goals.

Optimize Your Prices for Ideal Buyers

Believe it or not, you don't need to justify your prices.

Does your doctor? Are prices at your favorite fine-dining restaurant up for debate? No and no. If you told the server, "I never pay that much for dry-aged ribeye and Maine lobster," they'd blink at you. You'd soon be escorted out by the manager.

Your job is to charge what you consider fair prices and then deliver commensurate value. Your job isn't to mollycoddle your clients and manage what they feel. Their budget isn't your problem to solve.

A handful of clients, thinking only about their bottom line, not yours, may feel confused and stung by your price hike. They may leave in a huff. One prospect told freelance content and copywriter Beth Longman that her price per article was "insanity," though it was lower than the industry standard.[1]

More mature clients will understand why you raised your prices. Even while they mourn not being able to afford you, they'll applaud your pluck.

Make It Weirdly Precise

As you finalize your price, pick an unusual number. This advice comes from my own experience and this bit of reassurance I happily came across in *Never Split the Difference* by Chris Voss:

> The biggest thing to remember is that numbers that end in zero inevitably feel like temporary placeholders, guesstimates that you can be easily negotiated off of. But anything you throw out that sounds less rounded—say, $37,263—feels like a figure that you came to as a result of thoughtful calculation. Such numbers feel serious and permanent to your counterpart, so use them to fortify your offers.[2]

If Voss, a former FBI hostage negotiator, got better results with "less-rounded figures" in high-stakes situations, then freelancers can, too.

Here is my rationale for making my prices weirdly precise:

- Our brains resist uncertainty and ambiguity. Based on the way we're all wired, uncertainty implies risk and danger. One study even suggests that uncertainty causes more stress than knowing definitively that something bad will happen.[3]

- We feel better about making a bet[4] on something when we know more about it, meaning when we have more certainty.[5]

- We crave certainty at a subconscious level, and specificity enhances certainty. (You might say specificity is to certainty what salt is to steak.) Specific numbers make

NINE COUNTERINTUITIVE MOVES
FOR LIFE-CHANGING FREELANCE INCOME

a price seem more purposeful and come across as more trustworthy.

- A weirdly precise price hints at an equally precise process: "He didn't pull that number out of thin air before the call. He arrived at it through some formula or process."

Whether or not you think my logic is sound, I can tell you that making it weird has worked for me:

$575 or $625 for 300 words of web copy, not $500 or $650

$2,975 for a narrative, long-form case study, not $3,000

$3,375 for a 1-Day Brand Sprint, not $3,500

Try adding an extra $25 or $75 to enhance specificity. Those small, odd increments won't break the bank for the client or stall the negotiation, and they will add up to meaningful income for you over time.

Focus on Small, Incremental Gains

You may not be able to charge your Dream Rate all the time right out of the gate. You may discover that this aspiration, appealing as it may be, simply isn't realistic.

That was the case for one of my coaching clients, Myles. He used his Dream Rate of $150 an hour to calculate flat fees for several writing and branding projects. He got conversations going with potential clients and sent them quotes. Every single one balked at his prices, and he messaged me to ask me if he should compromise: "What do you think? Should I be willing to lower my rate for a big retainer like that, especially this early in my career? Or do I need to insist on the dream rate from the start to have a shot at a sustainable business?"

What I told Myles is that his Dream Rate was a reference point, not something he needed to defend tooth and claw like his precious baby.

Freelance pricing is like bowling with bumpers. Each project is a bowling ball, and your two rates, Survival and Dream, are the bumpers that form a barrier between the lane and the gutter on each side.

If you price a project too low and make less than your Survival Rate, you end up in the gutter with debt, back taxes, or both. I've learned this lesson the hard way—cough—more than once.

And if you go way too high and too fast with your prices, you're likely to get so many nos that you struggle to win any projects. Now you're in the other gutter.

The projects and prices you're able to get may zigzag between your Survival Rate and Dream Rate, but if you stay somewhere between them, you'll knock some pins down. You'll be playing the game better than most.

Edging closer to your Dream Rate puts you in a position to earn more, keep more, and save more. You can confidently turn down projects at or below your Survival Rate, break up with clients who become difficult, and finally get that Dolly Parton tattoo. The freelance trifecta!

Seriously though, any amount you charge above your past prices is a win. We compete against our past rates, not our future ones. We track our growth the way Dan Sullivan describes in *The Gap and The Gain*: "The way to measure your progress is backward against where you started, not against your ideal." [6]

For example, Emmy- and Telly-winning video editor Jesse Koepke opted for 10 percent increases: "If your rate isn't rejected, add 10 percent to your next project. Keep raising it until you find the ceiling."[7]

When in doubt, bowl your price right down the middle, between your Survival Rate and Dream Rate.

There Is No Perfect Price

We can bloviate about "competitive" or "market" or "dream" rates until we're blue in the face, but the truth is, freelance pricing is dynamic. The day you finally land on the perfect price is the day your needs change—again.

The right pessimistic *and* optimistic price is the one that moves you a bit closer to where you want to be.

Three approximate points on the freelance pricing continuum will help you determine just how aggressive you can be when pricing your next project:

1. Stability. If your freelance earning is unstable, your first earning target will be the Survival Number you need to pay all your bills each month and not accumulate debt.

2. Sustainability. If your earning has stabilized, then your next target is to bowl closer to your Dream Rate and start growing your emergency fund (and walkaway power).

3. Flexibility. Once you have an emergency fund to sustain you during leaner months, you can set your sights on more ambitious earning goals and more aggressive prices that propel you past modest creature comforts to true lifestyle freedom.

Phew. We made it past all those pineapples and bowling balls. You added up the time you really need for the project. You found your Pessimistic Price. You made it weirdly precise.

Remember:

- You can't manufacture more hours, so you must find creative ways to repackage your hours and charge more for them.

- You get your Pessimistic Price by picking a project, adding and rounding up the total time required, multiplying that by your Dream Rate, and adding a 20 percent buffer. Expect clients to be on their worst behavior, and price projects accordingly.

- If your prices aren't offending someone, you're undercharging. That said, you may need to focus on small, incremental gains. Any amount you charge above your past prices is a win.

NINE COUNTERINTUITIVE MOVES
FOR LIFE-CHANGING FREELANCE INCOME

- The clients and projects who got you to where you are won't get you to where you want to be. You may need to pivot to a new niche where people won't balk at your prices.

- There is no perfect price, but the right price will move you a bit closer to where you want to be.

You've got your new price. It is smart and strategic because it encompasses both your immediate needs and long-term financial goals. But how do you convince clients to pay that price? Pricing is one thing, and earning is another.

We'll cover earning in Part II.

Dear Reader,

Hey, Austin here. You have me to blame for this book's existence.

I set out to write a short, entertaining, and helpful book, and I hope you're getting a lot out of it so far. You don't want to miss the second part (Earning). Before you keep reading, I have a favor to ask.

Would you consider leaving a review for *Free Money* on Amazon?

My goal is for this book to become a staple in every freelancer's library, a business nonfiction classic, and one way you can help raise awareness is by writing a short paragraph about any new ideas you've picked up or how the book has helped you change your pricing and thinking.

Party on,

Austin Church

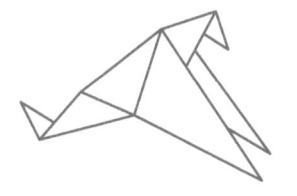

PART II:

Earning

"Charge as high a price as you can say out loud without cracking a smile."

—Dan Kennedy

MOVE FIVE:

◇◇◇◇◇◇◇◇◇◇

Find Your Next Three

ONE OF THE FUNNIER MISADVENTURES I'VE HAD AS A FREELANCER HAPPENED IN OCTOBER 2019. A software development agency had flown me up to Toronto for a two-day branding sprint and put me up at a Best Western in Newmarket across from Upper Canada Mall.

When I'm traveling, getting outside always helps me feel a bit more human—dare I say, more grounded? A quick glance at Google Maps revealed a park, nature preserve, and network of hiking trails behind the mall.

"Perfect," I thought. "That's where I'll head during my morning run."

That Thursday began as planned. My alarm woke me up. I put on my workout clothes. A jog across Yonge Street and through the parking lots led to residential streets and the splotch of green I'd seen on the map. I settled into an easy, ten-minute pace, and all was right with the world.

As woods gave way to more woods, my phone lost the signal. Was I even on Dave Kerwin Trail? I had no clue.

My anxiety began to ratchet up when I checked the time and saw that my thirty-minute run had stretched over an hour.

Being lost in a forest on your own time is one thing, even a good one at times. Being lost when a client has paid you five figures to help them solve a business problem and is wondering why you aren't responding to texts and calls is another thing entirely, and a rather embarrassing one.

By the time I finally took the path that took me out of Peggy's Wood Park, I had maybe fifteen minutes until Kostiantyn, my client, picked me up at the hotel. The maps app, suddenly so eager to serve, showed that I was still a good mile and a half away. Waiting for an Uber would take more time than simply running back.

I had to swallow my pride and send a text to Kostiantyn explaining how I'd gotten lost and turned a three-mile jog into a seven-mile slog. Then, despite being tired already, I hoofed it back to the hotel, showered quickly, and met Kostiantyn in the lobby.

He was nothing but gracious, we got the brand insights we needed that day, and I got a lesson about navigation in unfamiliar places.

Smart runners wear a GPS watch for good reason. They can't depend on cell towers for a strong signal. They can't always know what's around the next bend. A fork in the trail may offer a shortcut or detour.

When I was crisscrossing the suburban wilds of Newmarket, I had a destination in mind: my room at Best Western. However, when my phone lost the signal, the GPS was next to useless. It could show me approximately where I was on a map but not the turns to take or exactly how far to go.

Freelancers find themselves in a similar predicament. We know where we'd like to end up, with more money and freedom, a roster of respectful clients, and rewarding work. But exactly which turns do we take to get there?

Traversing the in-between can be so tricky. Many of us burn precious time dashing down trails to nowhere. To get out of the proverbial woods, we need a map and a destination.

What's It All For?

Now, some of you might be thinking, "You're killing me, Smalls. I don't have time for cute wayfinding analogies. Just tell me how to charge more already!"

Wayfinding is an odd concept in a freelance pricing guide, I'll grant you, but before you stock up on tactics, you might pause and consider, "What *is* it all for?" The extra money, I mean. Were you to finally, definitively, charge the prices you've dreamed about and start bringing home life-changing income, what would happen? What would your life look like?

Each of us needs colorful, textured answers to those questions. "More money" makes a crappy compass because it always symbolizes something else: safety, control, or status; mornings spent tending your garden; long weekends spent overlanding; or more time spent writing your fantasy fiction series.

Have you ever called a bank or telecom company to fix a problem with your account and been redirected three or four times? The first rep says, "I can't help you. I need to connect you with the Online Support department." The second rep passes you off to Fraud, but apparently, that entire department was out to lunch. The series of polite but pointless conversations makes you wonder if you died and went to customer support hell.

The thoughtless pursuit of more money is similar. It keeps referring you to another department. Money provokes more questions than it answers, as freelance writer and strategist Rachel discovered:

> I started freelancing full-time about eight months ago, after years of moonlighting, and I've grown my client roster really quickly. I'm actually at a full workload now and have as much as I can reasonably complete. My question is essentially: *now what?* Do I just keep raising my prices to meet supply and demand? Do I create a product? Do I just keep keeping on?" [emphasis mine][1]

Now what? What next? What is it all for?

These questions bubble up when freelancers reach a milestone, often sooner than we expect, and encounter not suave waiters passing out celebratory flutes of sparkling clarity but muddy cocktails of maybes and misgivings.

One of my coaching clients, Kellie, wondered if she could build a second, post-corporate career as a freelancer. Later, after she proved to herself that she could run her own business, a major financial achievement brought not satisfaction but burnout: "I had a $20,000 month, and it nearly killed me. I was miserable."

Josh, a former advertising strategist and fintech startup founder, started his own agency and landed a big project with Nike. That giant, swoosh-shaped aspiration culminated in what he labeled "bummedness." What was he supposed to do next? Go after an even bigger project with another iconic brand?

How do you decide what the next level up is? Is "up" the right direction? That question blooms into a bigger one: "What do I want?"

Freelancers want the basics, of course: life, liberty, and superbly crafted vanilla lattes. But beyond that, an honest answer may roam all over the place.

Here's mine: I want a deep sense of purpose in life, intimate relationships, physical safety and financial security, opportunities for my kids, continued good health, lots of trips and adventures around the world, and fulfilling work. I want to know and be known, to write books and eventually get an agent and book deal with a traditional publisher, to love God and to follow Jesus, to learn Spanish, to play the guitar, and to go to culinary school (if I want).

Hopefully, you now understand why you may need to get some clarity on what you want and what you want to do before you run headlong into the pricing and sales tactics. You can go make more money, but what's the money for? Here's a recap of why freelancers and consultants struggle to articulate what we want:

- Freelancers' interests, desires, and dreams are all over the map.
- "More money" is a crappy compass.
- Achieving milestones doesn't bring the desired satisfaction, a phenomenon psychologists call "arrival fallacy."
- Family, peers, ego, and culture tell us what we should want, and that cacophony can drown out our true desires.
- Meanwhile, we've still got to find work, pay our bills, and navigate the freelance landscape, ideally in a way that feels like progress.

What's a beautiful multi-passionate, multipotentialite freelancer to do?

I recommend four things: deciding where you are, marking your distant mountain, adding the magic word, and practicing disciplined simplicity.

Decide Where You Are

You've surely heard of the corporate ladder, but what are the career progressions for freelancers? After hundreds of conversations with freelancers, I've noticed four stages in the freelance journey:

- Moonlighter
- Hustler
- Lifestyler

- Diversifier

Each stage, or progression, comes with its own distinct set of motivations, challenges, mistakes, and questions. Peruse them and decide where you are. Take special note of which stage, breakthrough, and financial goal resonate with you.

Better yet, record what resonates in your journal. You'll want those insights a little later.

Moonlighters

Most freelancers I know start part-time by picking up freelance projects here and there while holding down another job. I use "job" here loosely to mean not just a full-time employment, but an entirely different set of obligations that consumes most of a Moonlighter's time and attention.

A designer may have a salary at a digital agency and create album covers and T-shirts for bands at night. A high school English teacher may pick up book editing projects during the summer. A stay-at-home dad may homeschool his kids and shoot ten to fifteen weddings a year.

Here's an unusual one I heard recently: My friend Matt's dad served as a senior pastor at a church, but several months a year, he'd put on his CPA hat and prepare tax returns.

The *motivations* here will be familiar to many of you:

- Testing the waters with the whole freelancing thing
- Making extra money on the side for fun, bills, or a big purchase

- Having creative freedom when a nine-to-five job doesn't scratch that itch

Moonlighting can start by accident, and your freelance business may grow organically in stops and starts. You started sharing your illustration projects online, and Aunt Barb surprised you with a direct message: "Can I pay you to create a holiday card for my recruiting firm?" That single project paid for all the gifts you bought that year and woke you up to the possibility of a side hustle.

Moonlighters have several main *challenges*:

- Finding projects
- Finding time and energy to complete the projects
- Juggling the responsibilities that come with managing a business

The small loaf of daily minutes must feed many mouths, but plenty of Moonlighters figure out how to divvy it up and are content to keep the side hustle on the side.

Moonlighters don't need many tools because you don't have many projects or tasks to keep straight at any one time.

The common thread among the *mistakes* they make is a muted sense of urgency:

- Undercharging, because they don't rely on the income
- Inefficiency and sloppy process because they don't have a tight production queue

NINE COUNTERINTUITIVE MOVES FOR LIFE-CHANGING FREELANCE INCOME

- More casual attitude toward building the brand and business—for example, having a weak web presence, out-of-date portfolio, and forgetting to ask for testimonials, referrals, and repeat business

Questions, fears, and insecurities vary with the person. Here are the more common ones:

- What's the next logical step for my business?
- How do I break into freelancing?
- How much should I charge?
- Where do I go from here?
- Am I doing this right?

The main *breakthrough* for Moonlighters is growing confidence in their ability to win projects and deliver outcomes while managing their other responsibilities.

The main *financial goal* for Moonlighters is socking away cash in an emergency fund, useful for its own sake in stabilizing one's personal finances, but also important for a longer financial runway if they were ever to go full-time freelance.

Hustlers

Eventually, some Moonlighters decide to take flight into full-time. The reason is often a growing dissatisfaction with a full-time job—the pay, coworkers, slimy supervisor, toxic culture, or unfulfilling work.

Other folks get pushed forcibly out of the nine-to-five nest. When I lost my job during the Great Recession in 2009 and suddenly found myself freelancing full-time, I had two choices: flap desperately to stay aloft like a drunken buzzard or sink like a stone. I always had an entrepreneurial bent, but I didn't notice and own it until I was in my late twenties.

Each of us is an iron filing caught between two magnets. I tried the more conventional path first, and the safety, security, and predictability of a regular paycheck appealed to me.

However, the pull of the mastery, autonomy, and purpose magnet (or MAP, *a la* Daniel Pink's book *Drive*) eventually won the tug-of-war. No one to answer to. No soul-crushing meetings or icky performance reviews. Glorious freedom!

Well, not quite. Every career path has its own set of problems. As a newly self-determined freelancer, I didn't have to listen to my old creative director remark on the holes in my jeans again. ("It's called style, sir. You might explore it.") But that didn't change the fact I had only $486 to my name.

In four short days, I went from "I really ought to save more" to "Shifurghk!" (That's the noise you make when your rational mind overloads with panic.)

The *motivations* of Hustlers are etched into my memory with the acid of painful firsthand experience:

- Winning more, better projects (i.e., ones with more budget and creative license)

NINE COUNTERINTUITIVE MOVES
FOR LIFE-CHANGING FREELANCE INCOME

- Selling services based on skills you already have like copywriting and design
- Not screwing up projects and embarrassing yourself
- Pretending you have a clue what you're doing
- Trying to be "competitive" with your prices
- Making enough to pay bills
- Serving clients well

Freelancing isn't a nifty experiment anymore. It's survival.

It's easier to hit a deadline when you don't want to flunk out of college or get fired, but Hustlers can't rely on the external scaffolding of a team, boss, and routine. The red cartoon devil version of your professor or boss no longer hovers over your shoulder and tells you to get back to work, and new *challenges* crowd in:

- Overthinking
- Perfectionism
- Procrastination
- Second Guessing
- Imposter Syndrome
- Scarcity Mindset (the biggest turd of them all)

Mistakes multiply like beetles on a dung pile:

- All the mindset traps just mentioned

- Shoddy contracts (or none at all)
- Offering every service, like a one-person bodega
- Undercharging (You keep telling yourself you can't afford to lose the project.)
- Weak boundaries with clients and enabling their bad habits along with your own
- No specialization and weak positioning: "You have a pulse and a budget? Let's roll!"

The burning *questions* for Hustlers are lit-up arrows pointing to breakthrough:

- How do I depend less on referrals?
- How do I get a grip on my marketing?
- How do I make more money without simply working longer hours?
- How do I raise my prices without losing all my clients?
- How do I specialize or niche down?

The main *breakthrough* for Hustlers is setting smart, strategic prices that reward their skill, efficiency, and expertise. Higher prices can and should coincide with a pivot from charging hourly to charging flat fees. The secondary breakthrough comes through establishing a morning marketing habit that makes you less dependent on referrals—and much more likely to get the clients you most want.

The main *financial goal* for Hustlers is paying themselves as much or more, after tax, than the salary at their last full-time position and beginning to fund certain lifestyle goals.

Lifestylers

I've coached a *bunch* of these folks who remind me of me, circa 2017.

You've hustled, and from the perspective of Moonlighters and Hustlers, you've made it. You're full-time. You've replaced the after-tax income at your last nine-to-five job and then some. That "Can I do this?" question no longer hangs in the air. You've proven to yourself and Bobby Boogerface that you can build an independent career.

That's not to say you've figured everything out. Oh no, the cracks are showing. If anything, the *challenges* are bigger, not smaller. New levels, new devils. And if you're honest, you toe the borders of Burnout more often than you'd care to admit.

Sometimes, you feel like a hamster on a wheel: find new project, deliver project, and get paid. Around it goes.

You've been fortunate, you know that, and you're grateful, you really are.

Yet, you can't help but wonder, "Now what? Is it ten, twenty, or thirty more years of this? Do I just keep raising my prices to meet supply and demand? Do I launch a digital product? Do I tell myself to be content?"

We freelancers can get so fixated on winning the next project, staying ahead of bills, and achieving financial stability that we become creative workaholics.

When you've been the freelancer who knows what it's like to have scary months, you may keep saying yes to everything. Surely, a little more cash in the bank will finally mute the anxiety and scarcity mindset that have squawked at you for years.

You tell yourself, "Just one more month's worth of savings in the emergency fund, and then I'll take my foot off the gas and start enjoying my life a bit more."

Then, scarcity mindset moves the target: "Just one more debt paid off and big purchase locked down, and then I'll start breaking up with the bottom 20 percent of my clients, start passing up opportunities, and start doing whatever it is that normal, balanced people do when they're enjoying themselves. Go on more vacations? Organize the garage? Grow basil?"

The core *motivations* for Lifestylers are more subtle and have shadings of fear, hope, and everything in between:

- Avoiding grinding it out with smaller, less lucrative projects

- Finding better work-life harmony and not letting work, even if it's often enjoyable, crowd out other parts of life that are just as important

- Learning how to make the same or more income in less time

NINE COUNTERINTUITIVE MOVES
FOR LIFE-CHANGING FREELANCE INCOME

- Finding out what's next because you're a multipotentialite who doesn't want to do just one thing and may not want your current "successful" freelance business forever

- Getting more support and delegate effectively... That's a thing, right?

The common *mistakes* go hand in glove with the motivations and attendant fears:

- Playing it safe now because in a sense you've "made it" and don't want to accidentally blow up the livelihood you've already got. You're more tentative and less decisive now than when you were a Hustler and had nothing to lose by throwing stuff at the wall.

- Sustaining your business with predictable work, to support your lifestyle, while also continuing to accept projects you find tedious, stressful, or unchallenging.

- Creating freedom for yourself though you rarely maximize it. You take less time off than many employees, and when you do go on vacation, you worry about your business. You cheat and check your inbox or take a call to appease a client. You seldom honor your vacation and gain the benefits of truly unplugging.

- Delegating. You've developed expertise, and because you're good at what you do, you find it difficult to believe someone else could do it as well as you. That belief makes it difficult for you to delegate, even though *not* delegating is part of the problem, of which you're well aware. So, you still spend too much time on $10/hour tasks, not $100/hour or $1000/hour tasks.

- Choosing prices that feed predictability but not necessarily excitement. Experienced as you are, pricing can still be a struggle. You want to be compensated for all your skill, experience, and expertise, but you're often up against less experienced but cheaper "competitors." Some clients use price for comparison, which isn't fair, but you don't always have a chance to explain why you're worth it before they make a decision.

The *questions* at this stage get more nuanced and existential:

- "What now?"
- "What do I really want?"
- "What do I want my life to look like?"
- "How can I make my highest and best contribution to my family, community, and world?"

You start to look for ways to diversify your income because, no matter how high you take your prices, freelancers and consultants still trade time for money. You want to weaken that link.

The main *breakthrough* for Lifestylers is getting better leverage through strong positioning, specialization, juicy offers, value-based pricing, an always-be-marketing practice and healthy pipeline, well-defined processes, and deliberate mindset upgrades.

The main *financial goal* for Lifestylers is hitting their desired monthly income target with fewer hours invested each week and seeing less fluctuation in earning from month to month, thanks to strategic pricing and consistent marketing. Consistent income creates a flywheel of saving more, paying oneself with "old" revenue, becoming more selective with the clients and projects you take on, and feeling more satisfaction overall with work, earning, and life.

Diversifiers

This is the stage where I am now. I've experimented with the four main ways that freelancers expand their businesses beyond selling their creative skills:

- Coaching other freelancers and consultants
- Charging value-based prices for consulting engagements
- Scaling up into a lean agency with a team of contractors and/or full-time staff
- Building an audience and creating one-to-many products and services to sell

Of course, Diversifiers, like Lifestylers, are interested in more than money, though a certain amount of money hits a pressure release valve. (According to a landmark study from Princeton University, the number is $75,000, or $100,000, adjusted for inflation. More about that study later.)

But what happens after you earn enough to cover the necessities and some niceties? How do you think about your work and career?

Diversifiers start optimizing for less dense calendars with more unclaimed time: time to draw, go on field trips with the kids, or travel without squeezing in productivity on the edges.

There's more to life than work, and more to work than money. Diversifiers also start optimizing for impact and true fulfillment. Things like "service," "impact," and "whatever happened to that children's book I wanted to write?" come into play.

The focus shifts from "how can I make this work?" to "what do I want my days and life to look like?" and "what kind of work would I do for free?"

It's no surprise that many freelancers who reach this stage want to give other freelancers a hand up through teaching, training, and coaching.

The core *motivations* for Diversifiers are as follows:

- Self-respect blended with creative license: "Either you let me do what I'm good at, or I'll find another client who will."

- Time affluence: "Life's short, and I want to do other things beside build my clients' empires."

- Diversified income streams: "It would be nice to be less dependent on service income."

- Desire to get better leverage, or better results with less effort. This manifests in both more tactical, short-term decisions to shore up positioning and create juicy offers and more strategic, long-term decisions to build an audience and own a direct relationship with them—

- for example, by building an email list and sending a regular newsletter.

- Helping peers find their way. Once your mindset starts moving from scarcity to abundance, you realize just how fulfilling it is to inspire and equip the next wave of Moonlighters, Hustlers, and Lifestylers.

The core challenge for Diversifiers is effectively starting over. Diversifying income streams and optimizing for time and better leverage, not more short-term cash, means embracing new business models. Your rich, varied experience and hard-won expertise doesn't necessarily translate as you go from being the seasoned freelance veteran to being the rookie creator, consultant, or agency founder.

What your business needs from you changes, too.

The uncomfortable responsibilities and lackluster results can be disorienting and discouraging at first: "I'm good at [insert your freelance work], so why aren't I getting better results with [insert next iteration of your business]?"

As you devote more time and attention to developing the business rather than simply delivering more projects, you may see a temporary drop in income. Diversifiers often misinterpret this lagging indicator: "I must be doing something wrong because I'm making less money, not more."

Despite their well-honed skills and deep domain expertise, Diversifiers make all kinds of *mistakes* while graduating to new business models:

- Not designing and executing experiments for what could be next because you've got so many competing priorities, and because it's hard to feel like a rookie again

- Building courses and other digital products *before* you've validated the offer with real people in the target audience

- Taking your eye off the marketing ball and/or letting communication and client experience suffer as you grow your audience and product business

- Starting new projects and ventures without first getting the support you need (i.e., hiring an assistant)

- Trying to build a team and delegate before you've clearly defined your processes and created standard operating procedures (SOPs)

- Overestimating how quickly you can build an audience and replace service revenue with non-service revenue (sponsorships, advertising, affiliate commissions, memberships, courses, digital products, and physical products)

- Needing to be involved with every aspect of every project (because no one knows it and can do it better than you, right?) and becoming the bottleneck that prevents growth

- Struggling to differentiate between reversible and irreversible decisions, not making the former fast enough, and developing a backlog of unmade decisions that clog up workflow

NINE COUNTERINTUITIVE MOVES FOR LIFE-CHANGING FREELANCE INCOME

- Wrangling imposter syndrome. Surprise! You didn't think it would disappear, did you?

Adroit management of all the details got you here, but that same tight control which served you so well now becomes the obstacle.

Unless you can trust others and create systems and processes that maintain quality and client experience—without your constant involvement or oversight—you block your own potential.

The *questions* at this stage have some of the same existential timbre as the questions Lifestylers ask (e.g., "What do I want next?" "What is my zone of genius?"), but they can get much more tactical, too:

- "What's most important right now?"
- "What do I need to start saying no to?"
- "Who can do this for me?"

You must let go before you can reach higher. You must decide which you want more: the comfort of control or the thrill of the entrepreneurial adventure, your own realized potential, and, yes, more money.

The main *breakthrough* for Diversifiers is getting leverage through consulting engagements and higher effective hourly rates, having a team that functions as an agency, and/or packaging up your knowledge and process sawdust as coaching and/or digital products.

FREE MONEY

Once you taste the white truffle of leveraged, non-service income, you can't untaste it.

The main *financial goal* for Diversifiers is replacing a big chunk of service revenue with non-service revenue. High-ticket consulting engagements may give you the warm fuzzies, but generating $1,000 or $10,000 with an automated email sequence feels even better.

Career progressions for freelancers don't stop with digital products. In his essay, "The Ladders of Wealth Creation: A Step-by-Step Roadmap to Building Wealth," Nathan Barry shares more of them.[2] Barry went from freelance design to digital products to founding and scaling ConvertKit, an email marketing platform, now valued north of $100 million.

My friend Stuart has taken the physical product path. After over a decade of creating videos for brands, he drew on his education in electrical engineering and background in content creation and designed a lamp with a phone clamp. The lamp provides perfect lighting for video calls and videos shot on your phone. Stuart sold his first lamp in February 2020, and his company, Canvas, has since sold tens of thousands.

You may have no interest in building a software company or physical products. You may love your freelance work and be perfectly satisfied with selling services. That's terrific. Seriously.

The last thing any freelancer should do, Diversifiers included, is blindly copy someone else or feel pressure to grow a bigger business or set a bigger goal.

NINE COUNTERINTUITIVE MOVES
FOR LIFE-CHANGING FREELANCE INCOME

Were I to airdrop my map, directions, and destination into your temporary camp in an alpine meadow, those wayfinding tools might help get you moving at first, but they'd eventually slow you down because you and I want different things. We want to end up in different places.

In an interview, Kevin Kelley, *Wired* magazine cofounder and the author of *Excellent Advice for Living*, explained why each of us needs a unique, personalized measure of success, not a copycat plan or set of numbers:

> Don't measure your life by someone else's ruler. I've had the privilege of knowing a lot of accomplished people, successful people, famous people, super-rich people, and man, the outsides do not represent the insides, and we tend to want to compare ourselves to their outsides, to their own ideas of what success is. [. . .] I'm better and I do better when I am not trying to imitate someone else's success state, how they define success. I mean, in a certain way, what you want to do is you want to kind of grow your own metric for what would be successful for you. And that is hard to do because we're kind of bombarded with images and suggestions about what would make a successful person. But if you talk to people who seem to have success you realize that you want to have a different metric.[3]

Amid so many competing and frankly discouraging images, how does a growth-minded freelancer develop the right measure? How do you decide which career progression you want or how to diversify your income streams?

You mark your distant mountain.

Mark Your Distant Mountain

Before you raise your prices and elevate your freelance business, consider how you want your life to look in three years.

To be clear, what you're after isn't your moon mission or what best-selling author of *Built to Last* and *Good to Great* Jim Collins calls a Big Hairy Audacious Goal (BHAG, for short).[4] Some entrepreneurs and corporations may need a BHAG to keep their teams enthusiastically rowing and growing in the same direction. However, as a company of one, you don't need to feel like you're playing small or settling if you don't have a BHAG.

In fact, the belief that you must start a movement or build a disruptive social enterprise or business empire can do more harm than good. Though no one comes right out and says it, freelancers and other creative entrepreneurs experience inertia precisely because we think we've got to have the ambitious plan in place before we take the first step.

It's fine to lead an ordinary life, wonderful really, but when I first founded Freelance Cake, I hadn't yet realized that. I felt compelled to sound my barbaric yawp from the rooftops: "I'm on a mission to help 1,000,000 freelancers make $100,000."

That number, one million, sounds impressive, and no doubt the bestowers of honorary degrees now have me on a short list because they saw my BHAG on my website. Yet would my life be any less meaningful and worthwhile if only 1,017 people attributed their life-changing income and its ripple effect to my stories and lessons, thinking and training? No.

We of comparatively modest vision don't need to feel pressure to be anything but our beautifully ordinary selves—no dented universe required.

The most helpful analogy I've found for thinking about this more common—dare I say saner—variety of vision-casting came from author Neil Gaiman's 2012 commencement speech, "Make Good Art."

He imagined a distant mountain:

Something that worked for me was imagining that where I wanted to be—an author, primarily of fiction, making good books, making good comics and supporting myself through my words—was a mountain. A distant mountain. My goal. And I knew that as long as I kept walking towards the mountain I would be all right. And when I truly was not sure what to do, I could stop, and think about whether it was taking me towards or away from the mountain. I said no to editorial jobs on magazines, proper jobs that would have paid proper money because I knew that, attractive though they were, for me they would have been walking away from the mountain. And if those job offers had come along earlier I might have taken them, because they still would have been closer to the mountain than I was at the time.[5]

My coaching work has revealed two truths about that distant mountain: Every freelancer has a different mountain in mind, and sometimes, it's more like a sand dune because it can change shape.

Wairimu, a nonprofit consultant living in Nairobi, has her Batian Peak (17,057 feet or 5,199 meters). She told me that making $25,000 or more per month will help her achieve financial independence and retire early in the next five years.

Zane, a senior copywriter living in Los Angeles, has his Mount Whitney (14,505 feet or 4,421 meters), and he told me about its different contours:

- Take weekends off.
- Do less admin work.
- Make $6,800 a month in pre-tax income.
- Bill no more than five hours a day, twenty hours a week.
- Take off a full day each week to provide childcare.
- Find the balance between consistency and some structured flexibility.

Neither mountain is right or wrong. Both are deeply personal, particular, and provisional. By "provisional" I mean that, as you get closer to the distant mountain, your perspective changes. As Zane enters the foothills, he may realize Mount Whitney is one peak in the Sierra Nevada range. His ultimate destination may change. Yours may, too.

Marking your distant mountain isn't deciding what you want to do or where you want to be forever. Instead, you pursue a minimum energizing clarity about what you want your life to look like in three years. As Cameron Herold notes in his book *Vivid Vision*, three years out offers "the perfect balance between realistic and achievable."[6]

NINE COUNTERINTUITIVE MOVES FOR LIFE-CHANGING FREELANCE INCOME

Minimum clarity will enable you to discern which opportunities represent smaller steps forward, sideways, or backward and which represent a tiger leap toward your distant mountain.

Seen from above, your progress toward that mountain will be more zigzag than straight line. Artists and entrepreneurs must embrace that inefficiency as a necessary part of the journey. Frustrating though they may be, detours and missteps teach us as much as leaps. We scoop up enough fresh clarity to illuminate the next step.

Whether your distant mountain is still shrouded in clouds, or you can already pick out the ridges, saddles, and rockslides, you will take more confident steps and make better decisions if you have some idea of where you're headed. Answer these questions to color in some detail:

- Work: What's the work you really want to do? (For example, Neil Gaiman had sampled enough work and sifted enough experience to know he wanted to write fiction, make comics, and earn his livelihood with words.)

- Finances: What is your next financial goal? What would you do with an extra $10,000? Or $25,000 or $50,000?

- Opportunities: What are your best opportunities right now? Can you identify any quick wins?

- Growth: What are your biggest obstacles or constraints to growth right now?

- Decisive Action: Is there anything you've been putting off because [insert excuse here]?

- Exploration: If you were to try something new in your freelance business, what would that be?

Once you've marked your distant mountain, you can take all the ideas you put down on paper and filter them.

Add the Magic Word

The key to gaining just enough clarity to take the next step with confidence isn't to go bigger and deeper with the existential questions that captivate philosophers, but to go much smaller by adding a magic, four letter word: "What do I want *next*?"

Most freelancers have diverse, often competing desires, ranging in magnitude from "I want pepper relish on my sandwich at lunch" to "I'd like to be financially independent by my fiftieth birthday." As a result, we pursue too many things at once.

I can't help but think of Dug, the dog in the Pixar movie *Up* who gets distracted mid-sentence and barks, "Squirrel!" Freelancers have no shortage of squirrels to chase, and much of our confusion, and the related blanketing sense of stuckness, has its root in scattered focus.

This isn't surprising, considering that so many of us are multi-passionate. We're not sure exactly what we want to do next, in part because we don't want to do just one thing. When the main money-making venture isn't going well or when a big milestone doesn't bring big clarity, we soothe ourselves with side projects, which both help and hurt because they divert attention away from both focused soul-searching and the need to take a definitive step, any definitive step.

I'm the last person who should tell you, "Focus! Finish! Be ruthless and ignore everything else!" That would be, uh, disingenuous because I've always got multiple irons in the fire, and if you told me to pick just one, I'd say, "Thanks, Dad, but that ain't happenin.'"

Yet, we can't advance toward the distant mountain while wandering in circles. Many a freelance career is littered with half-baked ideas, half-finished passion projects, and half-hearted implementation of a once-exciting growth strategy.

We need to make a wholehearted commitment to a path and stick to it long enough to see measurable progress or receive meaningful new input. In turn, these can bring the next dose of minimizing energizing clarity.

We need definitive answers about what's next, so we know what we're optimizing our freelance prices for. "Next" shrinks your landscape of paralyzing optionality to a narrower, more manageable field.

Imagine a dotted line between where you are and that mountain. What's the next aligned step? What about the one after that?

The word "next" enables us to prioritize.

In his book *Good to Great* Jim Collins examines the fundamental differences between companies that remain unusually profitable over decades and those whose performance is average by comparison.

One of Collins's key insights is that the great companies had no more than three objectives. Collins summarized his findings with this pithy remark: "If you have more than three priorities, you don't have any."

As a chronic over-committer, I don't like this insight one bit, no siree. I pile on goals the way a good deli piles on cold cuts.

Perhaps I could dismiss Collins if Gino Wickman, author of *Traction* and creator of the Entrepreneurial Operating System (EOS) hadn't come to a similar conclusion after working with thousands of successful business leaders. Wickman noticed that underperforming companies divided their focus across a dozen or more goals.

So here we have two heavy hitters who have studied remarkable executives and their companies coming to the same conclusion: the reason we don't meet our business goals is that we have too many.

Our root problem is those paralyzing options. Squirrels and chipmunks everywhere!

The solution is strategic simplicity.

Remember those notes you just made while reading about freelance career progressions and dreaming about your distant mountain? Use the magic word "next" to sift possible paths and priorities.

NINE COUNTERINTUITIVE MOVES FOR LIFE-CHANGING FREELANCE INCOME

Presumably, you're reading this book because you want to rethink your pricing. Perhaps setting smart, strategic prices is priority number one.

But where are you in your freelance career? Did the Moonlighter, Hustler, Lifestyler, or Diversifier career progressions resonate with you? What tiny breakthrough or financial goal will enable you to bring the next level a bit closer? Maybe you have the opposite problem: you need to start spending your freelance freedom in a way you're currently not.

Noodle on it and limit yourself to your Next Three priorities. Just three.

Write your Next Three down in your journal. Put them on sticky notes and slap them on the wall next to your desk. *Memorize* them.

Remember:

- Before you stock up on pricing tactics, you might pause and consider, "What is the extra money for?" Money symbolizes something else you want.

- Knowing where you are in the four career progressions for freelancers can help you decide what to do next.

- It's okay to not have a bold vision for making a dent in the universe. Instead, think about where you want to be three years in the future. Having that distant mountain will help you evaluate opportunities: Is this a step forward, sideways, or backward?

- The key to getting clarity and keeping up momentum is adding the magic four-letter word "next." Limit yourself to your Next Three priorities that deserve your focus right now.

See you in Move Six.

Some of you, like me, may have a weakness for journaling questions. I've sprinkled some throughout this book, but I've prepared a much bigger, shinier collection for you, along with a map to help you gather your thoughts. It's called The Wayfinding Retreat for Freelancers. Go to austinlchurch.com/free-money-resources to download everything for free. Enjoy.

MOVE SIX:

◇◇◇◇◇◇◇◇◇◇

Change Your Mind

WHEN I FINISHED MY MA IN LITERATURE IN 2008, I DIDN'T MAKE THE WISE DECISION TO LOOK FOR GAINFUL EMPLOYMENT. Instead, I burned through the last two installments of my graduate teaching stipend while gallivanting around Idaho, Montana, and Colorado with three friends.

The cans of Moose Drool from Big Sky Brewing and fishing gear from Blue Ribbon Flies felt much less essential upon my return to Knoxville, where I had no apartment, savings, or job prospects.

No one was hiring poets. How odd.

The parents of one of those fishing buddies offered to let me store my boxes in their garage and stay in one of their guest rooms while I figured out my next move. I picked up a few odd jobs, moving furniture and doing small landscaping projects, but I knew that wasn't sustainable. How was I going to afford the deposit for an apartment?

A call with my dad loomed in my mind like purple thunderclouds. We'd always had a good relationship. I didn't really expect him to say he wouldn't help me, so why was I anxious? Because his grown son, with a newly minted master's degree, had been a wee bit irresponsible, and we both knew it.

I'll never forget that conversation. I plucked up enough courage to dial his number and explain my situation as I paced the Doodys' front yard, back and forth, under an enormous elm. Eventually, I got around to inquiring if he and my mom might possibly help me out.

He agreed to float me through December, which I expected, but I didn't expect what he said next: "I wish your mom and I had done a better job teaching you and your sisters how to manage money. But we didn't. And now it's your responsibility to learn. After December, you're on your own."

Is it a coincidence that J. K. Rowling accepted an honorary degree from Harvard and made a remarkably similar observation in her commencement speech that same year? I think not.

Here was Rowling's take: "There is an expiry date on blaming your parents for steering you in the wrong direction; the moment you are old enough to take the wheel, responsibility lies with you." [1]

Knowing my father's habitual kindness, gentleness, and generosity, the moment when he set the expiration date must have pricked his heart. That moment is also one of the best gifts he has given me.

NINE COUNTERINTUITIVE MOVES FOR LIFE-CHANGING FREELANCE INCOME

No matter what I thought at the time, money wasn't what I needed most. I needed a precipitating event and a new story to tell myself. I needed fresh beliefs and expanded identity.

By the age of twenty-six, I'd already been in and out of debt three times. Several financial curveballs had contributed to this cycle. For example, toward the end of my first semester of grad school, my laptop's hard drive burned to an ozone-scented crisp.

How could I have gotten through finals without a computer? I had no savings to speak of, so I put a new one on a credit card.

An unexpected windfall enabled me to get back in the black, but by the end of my second year of grad school, despite getting a 30 percent income bump from my stipend and teaching associateship, I was right back in the same situation with an even bigger credit card balance.

Were "extenuating circumstances" truly to blame? No. My spending habits were.

The only predictable thing about personal finance is expenses we didn't predict, so the only way to not go into debt is to always spend a little less than you earn to leave some money in the bank. This is what old-timers call "living within your means." An emergency fund helps, too, or what the same old-timers call "saving for a rainy day."

Of course, I understood the concepts. At some level I realized I was being sloppy with money, but the poet in me was so enamored with living deeply and sucking all the marrow out of life that I never hardened the gossamer stuff of knowledge into practice.

I did, however, turn the wrong belief into identity. Physician and Dartmouth professor Dr. Paul Batalden said, "Every system is perfectly designed to get the results it gets."[2] All the evidence from four cycles of accumulating debt—a total timeframe that tracked with my entire adulthood—suggested I wasn't "good with money." That's the story I started telling myself, and if you tell yourself something often enough, you internalize it. Beliefs, whether true, false, or somewhere in between, become identity.

I unknowingly built a system of identity, beliefs, and habits that was perfectly designed to produce the results of short-sighted habits, anxiety about money, and credit card debt.

What could be more predictable than doing the same thing and getting the same results? Leave iron out in the rain and it rusts. Keep spending more than you earn, and you'll dig yourself into a deep, muddy, miserable hole called debt.

We can't outperform our beliefs, and I had believed that more money would make my problems go away. That come-to-Jesus conversation with my dad was the fingernail on the chalkboard I needed to break the self-induced trance. I started telling myself a different story:

- "I can raise my financial literacy."
- "I can learn how to be good with money."
- "I can form new habits that serve me better."

What story are you telling yourself about money right now?

Do you believe that someone like you can upgrade your beliefs, build a business you're proud of, and earn life-changing

NINE COUNTERINTUITIVE MOVES FOR LIFE-CHANGING FREELANCE INCOME

income? Do you find yourself eager to make that happen or secretly skeptical and backing away from the idea?

We must change our thinking before we can change our earning because unconscious beliefs influence how we show up. As Carl Jung noted, you can't transform beliefs until you make them conscious:

> The psychological rule says that when an inner situation is not made conscious, it happens outside, as fate. That is to say, when the individual remains undivided and does not become conscious of his inner opposite, the world must perforce act out the conflict and be torn into opposing halves.[3]

Here's the same idea, summarized and attributed to Jung (though I couldn't find the source): "Until you make the unconscious conscious, it will direct your life and you will call it fate."

Until you make your beliefs about money conscious, they will constrain your understanding of what's possible, and your decisions will fall in line with that smaller view of possibility. Your mindset is like an apple tree planted in a bonsai bowl of belief. The container constrained the tree's size, and therefore the fruit. Tiny apples cannot fully nourish you.

Enlarging your beliefs about money and your capabilities may take you months or years. This chapter will kickstart that process by helping you put certain beliefs about money on the table where you can examine them.

Rethink What's Possible

Beliefs must be examined and broken before they can be replaced. The writer in me hates the passive voice of that sentence, but the breaking of beliefs often happens to us. Think of an old belief like an egg, and a breakthrough moment as a tiny hammer that introduces the first crack with a *tink*.

Such moments catch us when we're looking elsewhere. A paragraph in a book makes you realize you gave up on art and need to start drawing again. A question from a mentor helps you put a mental finger on the edge of a growing awareness: you must stop doubting yourself. Perhaps you were sitting in the audience and listening to an industry expert give a talk and the insight struck you like a bolt of lightning: "This guy isn't that impressive. Why is he getting better results? I can figure this out."

Neuroplasticity ensures that we can, in a literal sense, change our minds, but we need abrupt moments of transition, cracks in the egg, to begin rethinking what's possible.

Or, to use a different metaphor: we need our rational minds to step outside of our automatic lives for a moment and to observe the beliefs and thought patterns operating in the background. Like Peter Pan, we need to pin down our shadows. We need to make the unconscious conscious.

Scattered across history you can find examples of what happens when beliefs change and psychological barriers come down. I'll share an example from running. Consider the record mile times from the first half of the twentieth century: In 1900 the record mile was around 4:15. In 1923, Paavo Nurmi ran a 4:10.4 mile in Stockholm. By the end of the 1930s, Sydney Wooderson had pushed the record time down to 4:06.4; and by the end of the 1940s, Gunder Hägg had shaved off nearly five seconds: 4:01.6.

When an English medical student named Roger Bannister ran a mile in 3:59.4 on May 6, 1954, he did more than set a record. After studying the mechanics of running and developing new training techniques, he proved a sub-four-minute mile was possible. Just six weeks later, John Landy ran a 3:58 mile.[4]

Here's another example, this one from space travel. Yuri Gagarin completed one orbit of Earth on April 12, 1961, and became the first human to journey into outer space. John F. Kennedy had taken office only three months prior, and the Soviet Union's accomplishment with Gagarin spurred Kennedy and the US space program to put a man on the moon and win the space race.[5] Would and could they have done it if Gagarin hadn't shown the world what was possible? That's doubtful.

Pick Positive and Negative Mentors

My friend Jay Clouse, host of the *Creator Science* podcast, wasn't necessarily expecting his unseen mental barriers to come down when he interviewed Marie Poulin in 2021.

At the time, Marie was earning $40,000 per month with her course business, Notion Mastery.[6] Jay knew Marie well, and she became a positive mentor who helped him reconsider his rules and limits:

I interact with her very closely, and when you know somebody well, who has a different money story than you, and you can see that they're not a different person than you, they're not doing things differently, they're not some superhuman with a different set of rules, it gets real for you, that your limitations are self-imposed in a lot of ways.[7]

Best-selling author and serial entrepreneur Alex Hormozi had a negative mentor. He describes a moment when he learned that another member of his mastermind group was making $350,000 per month: "He got up there [on stage], and he sounded like an idiot. Layla and I looked at each other afterwards and we were like, 'If he can do it, we can do it.'"

Negative mentors can offer a surprising source of encouragement and hope:

Seeing people who I didn't think were 'better than me' do something better than me gave me hope that I too could do it. I'd see somebody and be like, 'I don't think they work harder than me. I don't think they've got some genius brain.' If they can do it, I can do it, too.[8]

We all need those moments when a positive or negative mentor will crack our beliefs like so many eggs and prove that certain "true" beliefs are false and certain "false" beliefs are true. Only then can we recognize self-imposed limitations for what they are and burst through them.

Another thing that helps us upgrade our beliefs about money and our own capabilities as freelancers and entrepreneurs is better understanding how beliefs form in the first place.

NINE COUNTERINTUITIVE MOVES
FOR LIFE-CHANGING FREELANCE INCOME

Perhaps Your Single Best Opportunity As a Freelancer

Many people have a love-hate relationship with money, and many of the poets, writers, and other artists I've known were especially conflicted. In my creative writing program at The University of Tennessee, Knoxville, certain things were simply *understood*: We must appear erudite and cosmopolitan at all times. We must avoid sentimentality and seek originality. In pursuit of Art, we must elude the taint of filthy lucre and recuse ourselves from any and all conversations pertaining thereto.

The problem with this gag order is that money is an essential part of our lives. Money's many threads form the fabric of commerce in our local communities. They tie into our sense of safety, stability, and freedom. They intertwine our many wants and needs. Money isn't some superfluous patch we tear off and toss aside. Though it should never be our chief concern, it is important, whether we like it or not.

One set of beliefs and attitudes about money can constrain and mummify us, like so many strips of linen. Another set can liberate us. Therein lies the opportunity. As we examine our beliefs about money, we can unwind and upgrade the beliefs that aren't serving us.

Freelancers are particularly well-suited for this type of introspection because we're already accustomed to tinkering with our crafts and businesses. If we want to make meaningful improvements, we probe into what's working, what isn't, and where the best opportunities lie. (See also: the four stages of freelancing.)

Upgrading the system of belief operating in the background is perhaps the single best opportunity you have as a freelancer. No one is better than you at holding you back. The inverse is also true: no one is better than you at liberating you.

With that in mind, let's examine the false or only partly true beliefs about money most common among freelancers. I'll propose other ways of thinking that are equally or more true.

For starters, let's define key terms.

Money Scripts

"Money scripts" are our invisible, often subconscious beliefs and attitudes about money, and psychologists have begun exploring them. For example, in 2011, four researchers identified seventy-two money-related beliefs and organized them into four belief patterns:

1. Money Avoidance
2. Money Worship
3. Money Status
4. Money Vigilance

Then, they asked 422 people to say how strongly they agreed with those beliefs, couched in statements like these:

- "I do not deserve money."

NINE COUNTERINTUITIVE MOVES
FOR LIFE-CHANGING FREELANCE INCOME

- "Money would solve all my problems."
- "I should save money, not spend it."
- "Money is what gives life meaning."

The resulting study, published in *The Journal of Financial Therapy*, found that our beliefs about money hold significant sway over our income and net worth.[9]

Let's look at Money Avoidance. If you believe you don't deserve money, how likely are you to raise your prices at regular intervals? Not very. Undercharging creates short- and long-term problems.

Prices that are too low attract price-conscious clients. In my experience, bargain shoppers will squeeze out of you every last drop of work or productivity they believe they're owed.

What results is a painful cycle of getting stuck with penny-pinching, demanding, and demeaning clients, being short on cash, and feeling like you can't say no to the next client who comes along because the last low-paying project didn't help you get ahead financially.

No wonder some freelancers in the Money Avoidance camp complain, "There just aren't enough good clients out there!"

The Money Avoidance pattern can blind you to counterexamples right in front of your nose: Can you find freelancers with a comparable skill set who charge more and seem to be quite satisfied with their income and client roster? Yes.

What are they thinking and doing differently? More importantly, what do they believe about money? (This is where a positive mentor with a different money mindset can be so illuminating and galvanizing.)

The Money Worship pattern isn't a better alternative. If, without fully realizing it, you believe that money will solve all your problems, you'll make the wrong sacrifices in pursuit of it. You'll neglect your family, friends, and health. Like Hercules, you'll sever one of the hydra's nine heads, only for two more to grow back. Mo' money, mo' problems.

Until we examine and rewrite them, our unconscious money scripts make the calls and moves for us.

Where Do Money Scripts Come From?

Like other beliefs, we assemble money scripts with whatever material we have on hand. In *The Psychology of Money* Morgan Housel provides a succinct explanation:

Here's the thing: People from different generations, raised by different parents who earned different incomes and held different values, in different parts of the world, born into different economies, experiencing different job markets with different incentives and different degrees of luck, learn very different lessons.

I'll touch briefly on three places we acquire the stuff of belief: family, community, and society at large.

I already shared the story about my dad. He told me he wished he'd done a better job in the financial literacy department.

NINE COUNTERINTUITIVE MOVES
FOR LIFE-CHANGING FREELANCE INCOME

It turns out, my experience is fairly common. A couple of online searches for "financial literacy" and "youth" or "kids" will turn up a wealth of surveys and studies that point at parents' good intentions. They believe that children should start learning about personal finance sooner rather than later.

Yet, most families don't have matter-of-fact conversations about money. In the "10th Annual Parents, Kids & Money Survey" from T. Rowe Price, 64 percent of young adults reported feeling surprised at how little they know about personal finance. They didn't feel prepared to manage their money.[10]

The trend for decades has been most people, freelancers included, entering adulthood without the skills we need to make money, manage it, or talk about it.

Freelance illustrator Emily Mills told me that she was taught next to nothing about personal finance:

> My parents taught me to tithe and save. "Here's $5! Fifty cents goes to church, fifty cents to savings! They made me save up to buy my own toys, and when I was fifteen I got a job so I could save up to afford driving. My parents provided the car for free—they owned it, but I had to pay half the insurance and all the gas. They were good at preparing me for life and money, but they completely failed me when it came to personal finance. I never learned to budget, balance a checkbook, do my taxes, etc. No practical real-life money skills were taught. I wish they had helped me invest!

I've never forgotten the first sentence in Leo Tolstoy's novel *Anna Karenina*: "All happy families are alike; each unhappy family is unhappy in its own way."

Email marketing strategist Jay Sennett grew up in a "happy" money household. During a coaching session he told me that open, *healthy* conversations about money were the norm. Money was a tool, nothing more, nothing less. It could help you do things, but it couldn't make you happy.

My friend and marketing coach Ilise Benun had a similar experience, and she entered adulthood equipped with a matter-of-fact relationship with money. It's no surprise that Ilise wrote a book called *The Creative Professional's Guide to Money*. The subtitle says it all: "How to think about it. How to talk about it. How to manage it."

Many more freelancers I've spoken to experienced "unhappy" money households. Freelance writer and SEO specialist Liam Carnahan described his relationship with money as "finance-phobia" and explained how his family's "money bad, self-sacrifice good mentality" got him into trouble in his business and personal life.

Liam had to deliberately go through something akin to money therapy to reset his financial mindset and not feel guilty about making a living wage.

Filmmaker and video editor Jesse Koepke grew up surrounded by deal hounds driven by scarcity mindset:

> My family had a mindset of finding the lowest price, so now that I'm on the flip side I think I assume the person

is only going to go for a bid if it's a low price. Also playing into that is the fear of losing a project, or not having enough. (Probably another family mindset.) [. . .] It's been a journey in recent years of recognizing my beliefs, and now working to change them.

All our parents have belief patterns of their own, and in all fairness, they can't pass on healthy beliefs and practices that they never acquired themselves.

When I was kid, I overheard a family member say this about a wealthy friend: "We could live on the money they waste each year."

Without fully understanding the context or content of the conversation, I picked up on the emotional shading: The person talking was anxious about money, envious of what the friends had, and contemptuous of their perceived prodigality, all at once.

Now, here I am, decades later, recounting that moment to you. Out of thousands of conversations overheard, why did this one stick in my memory?

Because it became a part of a belief.

Kids constantly try to make sense of a world they don't understand. They're like magpies collecting shiny odds and ends to construct a nest.

My parents never sat me down and taught me the nuances of wealth, so I picked up the vague impression that wealth was suspect, and wealthy people were not appreciative or deserving of what they had. Most of what we believe as adults traces back to such snatches of overheard conversations, vague ideas we don't realize we're gathering, and stories full of gaps we tell ourselves about events in the past.

Even now, as I write that, a voice in my head whispers, "But isn't it true that wealth comes through exploiting others? The answer, of course, is yes, sometimes, not always. Yet, when hastily assembled half-truths have had years to cure in your belief system, they're difficult to pick apart, examine, and rebuild.

Our Communities and Cultures Also Supply Stuff for the Belief Nest

Maybe in high school you listened to your friends deride the spoiled rich girl whose daddy bought her a new BMW when she turned sixteen. Though she'd always been friendly to you, not snobby in the least, you absorbed the lesson: Having nice things can lead to ostracism. Openly enjoying wealth can make it harder to fit in. So, if you do ever have money or status, hide it.

Or perhaps you grew up as one of the rich (or richer) kids and the object of your friends' ridicule was the boy in secondhand clothes. His frazzled mom, chronically running late, would screech to a stop in front of school in her beat-up minivan, and the boy and all the siblings would spill out. His family's financial struggles made him the butt of jokes. You pitied him. You learned a different lesson: If you're ever in financial straits, don't show it. Keep up appearances.

Otherwise, you'll trade respect for pity.

I'm sure you've heard these truisms like these:

NINE COUNTERINTUITIVE MOVES
FOR LIFE-CHANGING FREELANCE INCOME

- "An honest day's work."
- "Money is the root of all evil."
- "Another day, another dollar."
- "Money doesn't grow on trees."

When we're young, we take such sayings at face value. A friend invites you to go to the mall on a Saturday, and you ask your mom for money to buy lunch. She gives you $20, and says, "Bring back the change. Money doesn't grow on trees."

We don't have the critical thinking to challenge their logic: Of course, money doesn't grow on trees, but fruit does. People love fruit, and fruit farmers make money by growing oranges, apples, and mangos. So perhaps money does grow on trees and you just have to run a profitable farm?

Time passes, and these feelings, impressions, and ideas about money become papier-mâché beliefs. They seem substantial, but they don't have any structural integrity.

The strangest part isn't that such ideas seep into our subconscious, but that we implicitly believe the opposites, too:

- An honest day's work." → "If you didn't work hard for the money, you probably did something unfair or dishonest."
- "Money is the root of all evil." → "Money is dangerous. It changes people for the worse."
- "Another day, another dollar." → "You've got to trade time for money, and there must be something wrong

with getting paid handsomely to do work that didn't take long."

- "Money doesn't grow on trees." → "Unlike things that grow on trees, money is scarce. For you to have plenty must necessarily mean someone else doesn't have enough."

I've had to dissemble each of these limiting beliefs by finding counterexamples and fuller truths. For every drug cartel feeding addiction and preying on weakness, there's an artist, writer, or athlete earning millions by entertaining and delighting millions of people. For every Bernie Madoff, there's a Warren Buffett. Both predatory and ethical enterprises exist. Theranos Inc. founder Elizabeth Holmes defrauded investors out of an estimated $700 million.[11] In contrast, since 1985, Patagonia has donated over $140 million in cash and in-kind donations to various environmental groups.[12]

In 2022 Patagonia's founder, Yvon Chouinard, went even further. He and his family transferred ownership of Patagonia, valued at about $3 billion, to a trust and a nonprofit that will ensure all its profits, as much as $100 million a year, go to combating climate change and protecting undeveloped land.[13]

The point is that you can find evidence to support whatever story you want to tell yourself about money and people with lots of it. At play here is a widely accepted and studied cognitive bias that psychologist Peter Wason described in 1960: confirmation bias.

According to research into confirmation bias, our beliefs will constrain what information we seek out and what plans we make.

NINE COUNTERINTUITIVE MOVES FOR LIFE-CHANGING FREELANCE INCOME

If you believe your freelance prices are constrained by what is "realistic" or what is "possible," based on supply and demand and other market forces, then you give yourself ample reason to keep your prices lower. Or, if you believe a freelancer like you can make a fantastic living doing work you love for companies you admire, then you'll look for ways to raise your prices and earn more.

One of the best ways to raise your prices is to mind your mindset. To make the unconscious conscious, as we've already discussed. To do that, let's examine five of the most common limiting beliefs about money that freelancers have and determine if they're worth unwinding and upgrading.

Money Script One: Money Just Isn't That Important

A theme has emerged across hundreds of conversations with freelancers. They choose slightly different words, but the meaning stays consistent:

- "Money isn't my primary motivator."—A freelance writer in a LinkedIn message

- "Money isn't important. Love, art, freedom is."—An illustrator in a comment on my Instagram post

- "Money just isn't that important to me."—A friend who invited me to coffee to talk about starting his freelance career

I know this dismissive attitude well. In my early twenties I had what I'll call a "conflicted" relationship with money. I have a vivid memory of reading T. S. Eliot's *Four Quartets* in the commons on Lipscomb University's campus. The dogwood and Bradford Pear trees were in bloom, and Eliot's words brought me to tears.

Was I content with the amount of money I made at the time? No. Did I want to make more of it? Without a doubt. Did I openly admit I wanted to make a lot of money? Absolutely not. I hadn't yet reconciled the poet and entrepreneur parts of myself. They were twin dragons, locked in mortal combat.

As time has passed, I've been able to subject old assumptions about money to more rigorous scrutiny by break them down into small pieces.

Here's how I approach the "money isn't important" idea:

- The last time I checked, I couldn't pay my utilities bill with a goat and a bushel of tomatoes. Most exchanges of value now happen with money, not bartering.

- As individuals living in modern societies, we need money to live, and if we need money for everyday life, then it is, in fact, important. Money is up there with food, water, and shelter.

- Does anyone really believe that money is more important than love or freedom? Of course not. No one on the sunny side of sanity believes that.

- Does anyone disagree that two things can have some measure of importance, at the same time—for example, my spouse and my children, my creative practice and for-profit business, my mental health and finances? No.

NINE COUNTERINTUITIVE MOVES
FOR LIFE-CHANGING FREELANCE INCOME

- Does anyone, given the choice, prefer a lack of money over a surplus? Other than monks, nuns, and other people who take a vow of poverty, no.

- I've never met a single artist, freelancer, or creator who was short on cash and content to stay that way. Most of us want more money than we currently have, and though we may waste some of it on luxuries, poor judgment, and vices—humans will be humans, after all—we also use some to do good in the world.

Money's implied or philosophical unimportance is a logical fallacy. Are many things more important than money? Of course they are! However, importance is a sliding scale with a timer attached.

What is important changes from moment to moment, day to day. Sometimes, we're more concerned with important, urgent things, such as paying our bills, than we are about important, non-urgent things, such as art. Mr. Eliot would agree that I can't feed my kids with free verse. I must rely on the commonly accepted means of storing and exchanging value, that is, cash and credit.

For human beings, urgency trumps importance all the time. When you have a full bladder and you're trapped in a crowded aisle on a plane waiting to disembark, you're not cogitating on solutions to world hunger. You're hoping that the closest bathroom in the terminal is very close and wondering just how much longer you can hold on before you pee your pants.

We freelancers don't prove our high-mindedness or moral purity by setting up a false dichotomy between one important thing (money) and other important things (love, art, freedom, poetry, you name it).

Furthermore, pointing out all the things that are more important than money doesn't quiet our anxiety. This bit of sophistry does harm because it shoves certain problems into the shadows. Your underearning or overspending problem won't magically disappear when you tell yourself money doesn't matter. It will only get worse.

Do you need to admit to yourself that money is important? Do you need to give yourself permission to want more of it?

Wanting more money doesn't automatically make you a morally and aesthetically bankrupt artist, freelancer, or creator. In fact, earning and keeping more of it will make you less of a burden on the people around you, and better able to support the people, communities, and causes you care about. Having more money may also allow you to level up your creative practice by buying supplies, taking courses, and blocking off time for retreats and development.

Whip out ye olde journal and ask yourself these questions:

- Why is money important to me?
- What would I do with more of it?
- What does money represent right now?
- How many of those dreams and ideas solely benefit me? How many of them benefit others too?

In his book *I Will Teach You To Be Rich* Ramit Sethi shares dozens of stories about what happens when people raise their financial literacy: They spend less time thinking about it, not more.

We must believe something is important before we will truly commit to mastering it and putting it in its proper place, literally and metaphorically. By giving money a place of prominence in your life and by giving it due attention—not adulation but practical respect—you can begin formulating a plan to earn more, keep more, and get ahead.

Money Script Two: Art and Commerce Don't Mix

Certain beliefs about money, art, and life aren't formed through a linear, reasoned train of thought and can be difficult to unwind.

"Art and commerce don't mix" is one such belief that has found its way into our cultural purse, along with other axioms like "pigs don't fly." The laws of gravity and the limits of porcine physiology don't leave us much room to argue, but what about art and commerce?

Without too much effort, we can find artists from various time periods, countries, and artistic movements who didn't profit monetarily from their talent, including these poets and writers: Zora Neale Hurston, John Keats, Edgar Allen Poe, Emily Dickinson, Henry David Thoreau, Stieg Larsson, Sylvia Plath, Franz Kafka, and John Kennedy Toole.

We can speculate whether Hemingway would have written or published as much without other sources of income, but it's logical to think that if he had been forced to spend more of his book royalties on living expenses then he would have had less to invest, and less investment income to live on later.

How much any artist makes *eventually* depends on how much they keep along the way. Other sources of income, including support from a spouse, enable some artists to spend more time honing their craft, spend less time on jobs required to pay bills, and save and invest more money along the way. This creates a virtuous cycle, both for craft and income.

The second factor I mentioned is timing.

In conversation for the *Daily Stoic* podcast, author Ryan Holiday spoke to author James Clear about the launch of their respective best sellers:

What if your book [*Atomic Habits*] had come out the day of a terrorist attack or my book [*The Obstacle Is the Way*] had come out the day of a hurricane and it just all got wiped away and you lost that moment? And you just didn't get it [the attention, momentum, and commercial success]? That happens, too.[17]

Both authors have sold millions of copies of books. Though good timing probably won't help a mediocre book, it can help turn a good one into a perennial best seller.

Artists vs. Freelancers

Now, let me tease out several crucial differences between artists and freelancers.

NINE COUNTERINTUITIVE MOVES
FOR LIFE-CHANGING FREELANCE INCOME

Artists produce art. Art moves and provokes, inspires and elevates, sobers and humbles, excites and entertains. Art is art because of what it does: Art elevates us through deliberate aesthetic experience.

The realization of that fundamental purpose can be simple or complex. A mural artist puts beauty where none existed before by turning a nondescript warehouse wall into a geometric mural. A satirical essay like Jonathan Swift's "A Modest Proposal" couches a critique of apathy toward the poor and eighteenth-century British policy toward the Irish, both justified on religious grounds, inside the absurd recommendation to turn children into food.

Like any other small business owner, freelancers provide a service, product, or experience. Some freelancers are artists, and they produce art for clients. For example, an apparel brand hires an outdoor photographer to shoot Yellowstone in winter. Other freelancers produce excellent, effective work to fix, enable, persuade, instruct, or sell. They solve problems for their clients. Art was never the aim for the UX writer who picks words that will make the client's software more intuitive to use or the marketer who puts together an effective strategy for a landscaping company.

In freelancing, aesthetic quality and efficacy aren't always the same.

You can succeed as an artist and create a thing of beauty that fulfills its purpose to elevate while also failing as a freelancer because the project you delivered didn't help your client meet her goal. The website you designed was pretty, but it didn't generate leads. The lush illustrations and eye-catching composition didn't get the job done.

From the client's perspective, there wasn't a fair exchange of value. Line up enough of these misses, and you'll struggle to get repeat business and referrals. Clients won't be willing to write testimonials. You won't have compelling case studies. Cash flow will dry up. Your business will fold, and not because "people just don't value art" but because the art was at cross purposes with the client's needs and business goals.

Some freelancers are artists, and all freelancers are small business owners. Until artist-freelancers place positive client outcomes above their own artistic expression and learn the essential skill of making money through a fair exchange of value, they will struggle to build a profitable and sustainable business.

Freelancers who are both artists and creative entrepreneurs must give themselves permission to acquire all three of the skill sets necessary to thrive:

- Those required for the art, craft, or discipline
- Those required to build a creative business
- Those required to keep and grow money

Believe it or not, this is very good news.

You don't have to be a once-in-a-generation, world-class talent with writing, filmmaking, design, illustration, development, you name it, to build a profitable freelance business. You just have to be good enough.

NINE COUNTERINTUITIVE MOVES
FOR LIFE-CHANGING FREELANCE INCOME

As long as your clients are pleased with the experience of working with you—how you manage the project and make them feel along the way, as much or more than the subjective quality of the deliverables listed in the Exhibit A of your contract—there's nothing the self-appointed critics and naysayers can do.

In "Make Good Art," Neil Gaiman encourages freelancers to not underestimate the value and staying power of being pleasant and punctual:

People keep working in a freelance world and more and more of today's world is freelance, because the work is good and because they're easy to get along with and because they deliver the work on time and you don't even need all three. Two out of three is fine.[18]

So, let's replace the worn "art and commerce don't mix" coin with a better, more nuanced set of assumptions you can bank on. Art and commerce do mix. Some freelancers are artists, not all, and all freelancers run small businesses. How much money you make long term as a freelancer has more to do with your business acumen, financial literacy, and project outcomes than with having a singular artistic vision or the likelihood your work will end up in a museum.

Artistic skills are especially valuable when freelancers combine them with other advantages: consistent marketing, strong positioning, juicy offers, well-defined process and timelines, and an overall satisfying experience for clients.

Let's end with an observation from one of my favorite artists and creators, Andy J. Pizza. In an episode of his Creative Pep

Talk podcast, Andy points out the biggest fans of "anti-money artists afraid of selling out": people who understand just how valuable artists and creators are to the economy and benefit from their ignorance about and hang-ups with money.

The solution isn't to martyr yourself for art or to ignore the many flaws in the financial system, but to take the measures you can and provide for yourself and the people you love:

> Having this anti-money approach is not helping us [artists and creators]. [. . .] This idea that I don't want to hear or talk about money, I see money as a bad thing—it is destroying you as a creator. And let me be completely and utterly clear: I am not saying that I think our economic system is fair or just, or that money doesn't complicate things. The money systems in our world are totally broken. I could not agree with that more, but we as artists, we still live and breathe and use the system that we are in right now. Take whatever measures to change things that you can, but until things change, our kids still need to be taken care of.[19]

The Danielle Steel Effect

What makes art "good" has always been up for debate. There simply is no pattern or prescription for artistic excellence or commercial success. You can find examples of critically acclaimed commercial successes, critically acclaimed commercial flops, and critically panned commercial successes.

Despite a "resounding lack of critical acclaim," all of Danielle Steel's novels have been bestsellers, including those issued in hardback. She claims the title of the best-selling author alive, with over 800 million copies sold worldwide.[20]

Are her books not "art"? Do they not elevate readers because the fiction is too formulaic? If Steel enjoys writing them and her fans enjoy reading them, does what critics say even matter? Where does that leave artists, freelancers, and freelancer-artists?

It simply isn't realistic to think that you can make a comfortable living creating whatever you like whenever you like.

Find your audience, give them what they want, and get the commerce side right.

Money Script Three: I'm Not Good with Money

Imagine a grown man tumbling down a hill, arms and legs akimbo. That's what my exit from academia and entrance into the business world was like in 2008, mostly for self-inflicted reasons. As I mentioned earlier, I had no money saved because I spent it all traveling. I assumed my problems would go away once I made more money.

Now, I see that my decisions, spending habits, and beliefs were really to blame. One specific belief tripped me up: "I'm not good with money."

Perhaps, like me, you have doubted your ability to hold onto money and use it wisely for any length of time. Shoot, maybe you really aren't good with money the way some people aren't good at cooking. Scorched casseroles for days.

The question is, what are you going to do about it?

Money is a concept you can understand if you want to, and managing money is a skill you can acquire if you want to. Looking back, I realize I was the only person preventing me from raising my financial literacy.

Excellent books and tools are available and inexpensive. Healthy, sustainable spending habits are within your reach, but you may have to change your mind and behavior before you'll utilize any of them.

In *The Psychology of Money*, Morgan Housel strips freelancers of the many excuses we make for ourselves: "Ordinary folks with no financial education can be wealthy if they have a handful of behavioral skills that have nothing to do with formal measures of intelligence."[21]

Ouch. Housel is right. People less intelligent than you with less education, more obstacles, fewer opportunities, and a low likelihood of significant bumps in income have cracked the whole "living within their means" nut. They save or invest the gap between their earning and spending. They get ahead a little more each month. Over time, those small gains add up.

I repeat, what are you going to do about it?

Some of us don't gravitate toward frugality and saving. I certainly didn't.

Some of us do not have a knack for budgets and spreadsheets. I don't.

Some of us didn't grow up in homes where open, non-anxious conversations about making, keeping, and growing money were a common occurrence. I didn't.

Some of us live in societies where significant consumer debt is the norm. Eighty percent of Americans have some form of consumer debt. Keep up with the Joneses. You only live once. Buy on credit. Pay it off later.

Maybe, like me, you enjoy life's finer things. So be it.

Let us still give our attention to the truths that empower us instead of limiting beliefs that bind:

- Nobody comes out of the womb already good with money. We can all learn how to make, keep, and grow money the same way we can learn how to cook, read, or ride a bike.

- Financial literacy, or making money and managing it well, is a core competency we can acquire, if and when we want to. Learn. Don't know how to grill salmon? Watch videos. Don't know how to do use free weights at the gym? Find a friend to show you. Don't know how to spend less than you earn? Fail forward.

- We can raise our financial literacy. We can learn how to be good with money and grow the gap between what we earn and spend.

- You've already gained other competencies and beefed up other skills. You've already learned how to do harder things. Why not financial literacy?

Financial literacy is equal parts knowledge, habits, and delayed gratification, but few competencies have more short- and long-term benefits or greater impact on your mental health, relationships, and overall well-being.

Are your spending habits wreaking havoc on your financial stability, growing your debt, and causing anxiety? Do you consistently spend more than you earn? Is your current level of financial literacy blocking your growth as a freelancer?

There's hope for you and me. Acknowledging the problem is the first jelly-legged step down that honeysuckle-scented trail to stability.

Money Script Four: More Money Might Make Me Greedy

Before we get into everyone's favorite cocktail hour topic, greed, I want to make several matter-of-fact observations about money.

For starters, money is confusing. Many parents do not talk openly about it with their children or teach them real-life money skills. Through osmosis, many of those children, who later become

NINE COUNTERINTUITIVE MOVES
FOR LIFE-CHANGING FREELANCE INCOME

freelancers, get the impression that money is not something to be proud of—or worse, that money is something to be ashamed of.

Money can change our perceptions of people and hurt relationships, yet people need money to live. Money can bring out the worst in some people and the best in others. Money won't solve all your problems, but it will solve your money problems. These conflicting ideas are like so many shopping carts zipping around in the grocery store of your mind. They're bound to collide.

Money is a tangible object and intangible concept. We meet our physical needs by buying things with physical bills and coins, and meanwhile, those objects symbolize past mistakes and future fears, simmering frustrations and nascent dreams. Money represents what we do and don't want, the lifestyle we can or can't live.

Money is emotional. It scares some freelancers and creators, both the idea of having too much of it and having too little. We're afraid to keep it—what will people think?—and afraid to spend it—what will people say?

Money is confusing, conflicting, physical, symbolic, and emotional all at once, and when you toss into the mix widespread financial illiteracy, we-don't-talk-about-it taboo, and experts who can't seem to agree, it's no surprise that we push ourselves away from the table. The stew has too much salt. It's inedible.

To be in a different, healthier place financially a year from now, you must sit back down and recommit to the subject of money. The first positive move we can make toward a wholesome understanding is giving ourselves permission to learn about money and replace the stigma with curiosity.

What is true, partly true, or false about it?

Take, for example, the belief that more money can make a person greedier. Money doesn't *make* you anything: greedy or generous, happy or miserable, peaceful or anxious. Money amplifies what's already there.

My friend Jon got a Porsche when he turned sixteen. The Porsche didn't make him reckless, but his own desire to take risks did. When he spun out doing 140 miles an hour, the Porsche was the unwitting accomplice, not the instigator. Money doesn't change make people greedy any more than fast cars make teenage drivers stupid.

Money is a tool, like a car or a knife. Does a cleaver make a chef dangerous? Is a surgeon with a scalpel menacing? Tools and circumstances draw out a person's character, personality, and potential, both the good and the bad.

For the record, money isn't the only such amplifier. Fame, status, power, age, pain, fatigue, and fear also illuminate what's in us. That pop singer didn't become a diva *after* her music took off. The offensive old man didn't drop his filter because of jowls and liver spots. A lottery winner didn't become a philanthropist the moment the giant payout hit her bank account.

Amplifiers and circumstances make our vices and virtues more obvious. My grandmother, who is one of my heroes, was patient, gentle, and generous when she was a young woman. Age has improved her best qualities.

NINE COUNTERINTUITIVE MOVES
FOR LIFE-CHANGING FREELANCE INCOME

Anyone who struggles with greed and pursues wealth in a way that sacrifices fairness, honesty, and the greater good, not to mention their own physical, mental, and spiritual health, will see that unhealthy attachment grow and calcify, until, like Ebenezer Scrooge, their heart changes.

Greed is a vice that can color our paradigm like a drop of green dye in a glass of water. What a generous giver calls hoarding, a miser calls insurance. Greedy people don't think of themselves as greedy. For them "greed" masquerades as something else, such as entitlement ("It's what I deserve"), winning ("We can't all be winners"), or a Darwinian pragmatism ("It's the wolves versus the sheep, and I'm a wolf").

Our behavior cascades from our paradigm, so if you're concerned about being greedy, then the concern itself signals your value for fairness, decency, and even generosity. Sure, you'll be selfish and lack restraint from time to time. You'll waste money you should have saved, and you'll splurge on yourself when you might have assisted others.

We all occupy different spots on the selfishness continuum, from one day and moment to the next. Even selfishness has a bright side: it's a beautiful self-preservation mechanism. (Have you ever observed newborns? They don't give a basket of beans for their parents' needs.)

The point is that more money will simply make you more of what you already are.

Most freelancers, consultants, and creators I've spent time with have big plans for what they'd do with more money. Those plans always include how they will surprise, serve, and bless other people, not because I prompted them to think beyond themselves, but because being good and doing good feels good.

Investigate the science sometime: doing good and giving money away releases oxytocin, and lo and behold, oxytocin, the "love hormone," is good for our physical, emotional, and social health.

For most freelancers, more money doesn't mean more greed. More money means more good accomplished.

Money Script Five: I Should Be Content with What I Make

Contentment is an admirable quality, don't you think?

My friend Eric once exclaimed, "I love my job!" He was making good money with good coworkers on a good schedule. Obviously, I was thrilled for him. I sincerely wish everyone had Eric's deep, thrumming satisfaction with their work and financial situation, but that's usually not the case.

Human beings are wired to want more. Since the 1960s, neuroscientist Jaak Panksepp has been studying humanity's seven most basic, or primal, emotions. The emotion he calls "seeking" appears in the list alongside anger, fear, pleasure/lust, care, panic-grief, and play. Panksepp believes that seeking drives us more than any of the others.[22]

The downside to seeking is that it doesn't stop. Even passing major milestones or winning the lottery won't precipitate long-lasting changes in happiness.[23] In his 2004 TED talk, Harvard psychologist Daniel Gilbert went so far as to say, "If it happened over three months ago, with a few exceptions, it has no impact on our happiness."[24]

Woof.

In her book *The How of Happiness* Dr. Sonja Lyubomirsky, professor of psychology at The University of California, Riverside, explores the factors that affect our happiness. According to Lyubomirsky, genetic makeup accounts for about 50 percent; everyday thoughts, attitudes, and actions for 40 percent; and circumstances for the last 10 percent.[25]

Spiritual masters across continents, religions, and millennia have made similar observations about the tenuous connection between circumstances and contentment. Around 62 AD, Saint Paul wrote this in a letter to the church in Philippi: "I have learned to be content whatever the circumstances. I know what it is to be in need, and I know what it is to have plenty. I have learned the secret of being content in any and every situation, whether well fed or hungry, whether living in plenty or in want."[26] Buddha said, "Contentment is the greatest wealth."[27]

Did I listen to the psychologists and sages? I'll give you one guess.

For years, I was obsessed with paying off my family's pile of credit card debt, business loans, and back taxes—$113,603, to be precise. I fell prey to the "Once we . . ." milestone thinking and allowed it to sabotage my day-to-day contentment.

When that pile-shaped absence finally came to pass in July 2021, my friend Nic asked me, "How do you feel?"

"I don't feel much of anything," I replied. The effervescent, whooping-and-hollering joy I had expected was nowhere to be found.

So yeah, I'd be the first person to tell you to practice contentment in the present moment. You can certainly pursue more money, but don't be surprised when the extra income doesn't have you leaping and kicking your heels long term. The target will have already moved. Your inner seeker will already be trained on a new mirage.

Now, I can already hear some of you interrupting my homily on contentment to say it's hard to be content when bills aren't getting paid and you're falling further behind, not getting further ahead.

Am I proposing that you be content forever with barely scraping by?

No. I recommend that you proactively improve your financial situation. Some freelancers need to make more money, plain and simple, and that's one reason I wrote this book, not another one.

We're talking about a both/and scenario, not an either/or: cultivate contentment, as best you can, *while you also work* toward financial stability and surplus.

NINE COUNTERINTUITIVE MOVES
FOR LIFE-CHANGING FREELANCE INCOME

The work of Dr. Angus Deaton and Dr. Daniel Kahneman provides helpful nuance here. From 2008 to 2009, they analyzed responses to the Gallup-Healthways Well-Being Index (GHWBI). Their research found that happiness results from two distinct but connected psychological states or sentiments people have about their lives: emotional well-being and life evaluation.

1. Emotional well-being is the emotional quality of one's daily and primarily social experience. Are you spending time with people you like?
2. Life evaluation is a person's view of the life she has led. Looking back at your life, are you pleased with what you have accomplished?

Kahneman summarized their findings this way: "What improves people's emotional well-being is different from what it takes to make them say that they're satisfied with their life."[28]

Can you guess which of the 450,000 respondents scored themselves lower on both life evaluation and emotional well-being? Those with less than $75,000 in annual household income, or, closer to $100,000 in today's dollars.

Deaton and Kahneman weren't exactly sure why the $75,000 (or $100,000) mark was so significant, though Deaton speculated, "Not having enough money to live a decent life really gets in the way of doing the ordinary things that make people happy."

Above $100,000 the relationship between income and emotional well-being breaks down. The name of Deaton-Kahneman study says it all: "High income improves evaluation of life but not emotional well-being."[29]

They have a point. None of us need search very far to find a wealthy, accomplished, and yet unhappy person.

So, what are the biggest takeaways for freelancers?

- "Just be content with what you make" is flimsy advice for those of us who live in a society where money is the primary mechanism for exchanging value. You just can't do certain things without a surplus of it: save for a house, buy reliable transportation, get high-quality healthcare, build an emergency fund, travel, or invest in your creative and professional development.

- The freelancers with the most emotional well-being *and* life satisfaction are the ones who spend lots of time with family and friends, consistently achieve their goals, and earn enough to live a "decent life," which means around $100,000 for people living in the United States.

- Once you pass $100K, don't expect your happiness or contentment to keep rising with your income. Most of us will keep moving the target until we become aware that's what we're doing. Twice as much money and stuff doesn't make us twice as happy. The thrill of material things quickly dissipates. Last month's new cashmere sweater becomes this month's barely noticed closet denizen. It's called "hedonic adaptation."

- Though you can't change your genetics, you do hold sway over your environment and external circumstances, and you can upgrade your everyday thoughts and behavior.

NINE COUNTERINTUITIVE MOVES
FOR LIFE-CHANGING FREELANCE INCOME

Better books than this one can give you strategies for reining in your spending while you also cultivate the spiritual practices that do contribute to contentment, namely, gratitude, generosity, and thriftiness. (Considering that everyone from Socrates and Confucius to King Solomon and Benjamin Franklin have lauded thriftiness, maybe we should investigate.)

And just to be clear: precisely whom do you serve by making less as a freelancer than you could? Reminding yourself to be content because others have less doesn't make you a more compassionate or empathetic person.

The best thing you can do for people in need is to help them right now, and the second-best thing you can do is put yourself in the financial position to help them more in the future. We can't give what we don't have. We must create the abundance before we can redistribute it. Enriching yourself above $100,000 won't make you much happier, but more generosity just might.[30]

Dr. Lyubomirsky would tell you that the key that unlocks sustained, long-term happiness is changing your thoughts, attitudes, and actions: "Thus the key to happiness lies not in changing our genetic makeup (which is impossible) and not in changing our circumstances (i.e., seeking wealth or attractiveness or better colleagues, which is usually impractical), but in our daily intentional activities."[31]

B all means, give yourself permission to make the money you need to live a decent life. Remember to practice contentment along the way. The feeling of happiness will come and go, but the spiritual practice of contentment represents true wealth.

Closing Thoughts

By now you know that the very idea of "money" comes loaded with all sorts of cargo, especially our desire for respect, safety, stability, fun, good health, long life, freedom, meaning, and an unambiguous sense of belonging.

Money becomes a vault of insecurity, shame, and fear. Both the lack of money and the fear of its loss cause anxious speculation about those desires going unmet. Most of us are either afraid to make too much and keep too much or make too little and have nothing to spare.

You can't outperform your beliefs. They either speed you to where you want to go, like a bullet train, or they slow you down, like a slog through a swamp.

Until you determine what memories, stories, and beliefs drive you, the next higher level of entrepreneurship and financial freedom will elude you.

One moment of great pride in my life came in April 2010 in a P. F. Chang's parking lot in Franklin, Tennessee. I'd met a girl. Things had gotten serious. I'd driven from Knoxville to Nashville to go ring shopping with my parents, and before we started the surreal experience of peering through glass cases in jewelry stores, we went to lunch.

I surprised my dad by handing him a check for $1,500—every penny of what my parents had loaned me in the fall of 2008.

At first, he stared blankly at what I'd put into his hands. I'm sure he'd never expected to see that $1,500 again. Such is the life of generous parents around the world. But the look of confusion quickly gave way to a smile that spread across his whole face. This moment represented a turning point in our relationship.

He had the proof in his hands that a man had replaced the boy and the twenty-something guy. I had kept my word to him and had taken responsibility for my actions and mistakes. Each month, I was earning more than enough as a freelancer. My finances were under control. I had started saving, and now I was paying off the last of my debt.

If you haven't had too many moments like that, keep going. Now is the time to raise your financial literacy and develop a healthy relationship with money.

Many of us must change our thinking before we can change our earning. I've been there, friend, truly I have. If I can change, so can you. This work may take you months or years, but starting it now means the best is yet to come.

Remember:

- Money is important. Art and commerce do mix. You may not be good with money yet, but you can learn how to raise your financial literacy.

- Money doesn't make you greedy, but it does amplify what's already inside of you. For most freelancers, more money doesn't mean more greed. More money means more good accomplished.

- Lots of people are worse off than you. That's not a good reason to make less money than you could, enough to live a decent life. The spiritual practice of contentment will contribute more to your life than more money.

- Take this opportunity to go down to the basement of your subconscious and put the dusty boxes on the rickety card table. What memories and moments come to mind? Write them down. Become acquainted with them. Make the unconscious conscious.

- Determine what it is you believe about money through messy reflection and journaling. Then, look for counterexamples. Ask yourself what else may be true or truer.

- Find positive mentors. Talk to other freelancers and find peers with similar ethics and values who clearly don't share your self-imposed limitations.

- Find negative mentors. Who is someone you don't admire who has already achieved the financial success you want? Let that bozo bother you. If they can do it, why not you?

- Read books and raise your financial literacy on purpose. Check out the list in the resources section at the end of the book. Pick one. Underline the most important bits. Take notes. Make a plan based on what the author recommends. You'll be gobsmacked at the difference six months can make.

- Identify new habits that will serve you better. Discipline is remembering what you want. Keep lowering the

NINE COUNTERINTUITIVE MOVES
FOR LIFE-CHANGING FREELANCE INCOME

commitment bar until the habit sticks. Then, increase the commitment.

See you in Move Seven.

Want twelve questions to figure out your money beliefs? Go to austinlchurch.com/free-money-resources.

MOVE SEVEN:

Take Your Vitamins

ON FRIDAY, MAY 1, 2009, I WALKED PAST THE OFFICE OF THE MARKETING AGENCY WHERE I'D LAST WORKED, TWO WEEKS PRIOR, AND UP A FLIGHT OF STAIRS. Though I didn't know it at the time, I was leveling up metaphorically, too.

A veteran freelance copywriter and agency owner named Andrew Gordon had agreed to meet with me.

I sat across his desk and reminded myself to breathe as he thumbed through the portfolio I had printed out. It seemed thin in his hands. Had six months at the agency been enough time to turn a poet and fiction writer into a competent copywriter? Doubtful.

Andrew looked up from the sheaf of papers, looked me in the eyes, and asked, "What's your freelance rate?"

"Oh, we're getting to the money already," I thought. This could get dicey.

"$40 an hour," I said. Praise God my voice didn't crack.

He considered that for a moment. "Do you mind if I give you some advice?"

Here we go, I thought. He's going to tell me to charge less, and I'm going to do it because I have no clue what I'm doing. I'm desperate. Somehow, I've got to scrape together $1,100 this month.

"Uh, sure," I replied. (I've always been known for my poise and eloquence.)

"If I were you," Andrew said, "I'd raise your rates to $75 an hour, effective immediately. Your work is actually pretty good, but at $40 an hour you won't be taken seriously in larger markets like Charlotte, Nashville, and Atlanta."

To say I was thunderstruck would be an understatement.

I'd just been pushed forcibly out of the nine-to-five nest when my old boss had cut the agency's staff in half. The agency had billed out my time at $85 an hour, and I reasoned that anyone who hired me would get twice the work for the same price.

What a bargain!

I hadn't considered that my affordable, "competitive" rates would signal a lack of experience, confidence, and skill—the exact opposite of what I wanted.

The clients I wanted wouldn't see me as a bargain because they would never consider me in the first place!

I never recovered from that conversation with Andrew in the best possible way. The idea was new, but I could *feel* the truth of it. I wouldn't command Rolex respect at Timex prices.

I did raise my rates soon after, and I credit Andrew with making me over $100,000 in extra fees that day. He might as well have handed me a Golden Suitcase when he handed me the lesson. Pricing is branding. Pricing is positioning.

Having smart, strategic prices is one thing. Knowing the Golden Suitcase strategies, tactics, and principles that enable you to land projects at those prices is another.

Sustained success with pricing hinges on a keen understanding of people, both your clients and yourself, and sound judgment and discernment as you navigate the ticklish situations and intriguing opportunities that come along.

When do you agree to a little favor for a client and not raise a stink about it? And when do you call the bigger "favor" what it is, scope creep, and notify the client about the extra cost?

Freelancers encounter many situations like these for which we have no neat, easy answers. A favor can establish bad precedent. Before long, you're doing all kinds of extra work for that client for free because you gave an inch and the client took a mile. A favor can also create goodwill. A fifteen-minute investment in the relationship paid dividends through $10,000s in follow-on projects.

This chapter will equip you with some of my best thinking at the intersection of pricing and business strategy. Underline anything that strikes you as wisdom worth internalizing—

what I call "vitamins." Start building your medicine cabinet of business principles to live by. Lay by your own collection of Golden Suitcases.

Tactics come and go; principles endure.

Better Questions Lead to Bigger Proposals

Most clients believe they already have clarity, but in my experience maybe three in ten can explain the project succinctly and rattle off a quick list of desired outcomes.

Closer to 70 percent paint their initial request in broad strokes.

Simply slapping a price tag on that initial request sets freelancers up for frustration later when the target moves mid-project or when we successfully deliver the wrong project.

Have you ever fulfilled a contract down to the letter only for the client to still be dissatisfied because they didn't get the results they needed most?

That dissatisfaction tends to ricochet. The client aims it at the real project—that is, at the deeper problems they didn't articulate and the expectations they didn't express—but the dissatisfaction bounces off and hits you.

You did what you said you'd do, yet if the project "feels" unsuccessful, you take some of the blame. Most clients don't hold you responsible for their lack of clarity consciously, any more than they consciously conclude a restaurant isn't good after ordering the wrong entrée. Yet, these vague impressions stick all the same.

Clients are responsible for managing their own feelings. Full stop. However, I had to learn the hard way to think more strategically: How can I preempt sour impressions that will come later if I simply agree to the initial request?

I now draw out the discovery phase rather than rushing headlong into a quote. We're only talking another forty-five or ninety minutes, not hours or days, which I spend pulling out buried insights and needs, with the help of better questions:

- "If you could wave a magic wand, what would happen in your business?"
- "What will a new logo give you that you don't have now?"
- "What are you hoping a new website will do for you?"

Think of a buried dartboard. Before contacting you, the client threw a dart and hit what they thought was the center: "This is what I want." However, as you help them uncover all the edges, both of you see that the dart hit a small green and black patch in the upper right. The initial request was nowhere close to the red bullseye, that is, the real project.

One specific client situation comes to mind. A marketing director asked for a quote for a new website. During our discovery call, I sensed that we weren't looking at the whole dartboard. I proposed a paid, formal project road-mapping session. She accepted, and we identified various other needs and wants, including "strong web presence," "telling our story well," and "being more competitive in our market."

Eventually, we dug down to the raw needs and root causes. For example, the CEO had confused a marketing vehicle (a website) with an actionable marketing roadmap and had tasked the market director with updating the vehicle.

The marketing director and I created a more logical, holistic roadmap. It made a case for the highest and best use of any marketing budget. Relatively simple and inexpensive updates to the existing website might suffice, and better strategy and planning would surely help them avoid the situation where they burned the entire budget on a pretty website yet achieved no marketing momentum.

Uncovering the dartboard instead of pricing out the initial request takes discipline.

You must be willing to risk a client's temporary irritation with your slowness or thoroughness to verify that the initial request is the real project. Small displeasure now, big gratitude later.

Delayed gratitude is the better business strategy, and your early discipline with uncovering the buried dartboard will consistently produce more needs and bigger proposals to match.

Asking better questions also makes it easier to quantify the value of the outcomes. For example, a client who asks for a website may really need more leads and a predictable process for getting them.

It's only natural for you to ask, "So how many leads do you currently get from your website? And how much is a new lead worth to you?"

If you're confident you can help them get an extra twenty-five to fifty leads over twelve months, or $250,000 to $500,000 in value, then a $25,000 website would represent only 10 percent on the low-end. A no-brainer investment for a value-focused client, right?

If you don't already have a list of thoughtful questions for uncovering the buried dartboard or bigger opportunity, go here to get my tool kit of twenty-two consulting questions for free: austinlchurch.com/free-money-resources.

Get Closer to the Money

The closer you are to the money on the client side, the easier you'll find it to charge based on the value you create.

A pay-per-click (PPC) ad manager is closer to the money than the designer handling the ad creative. The manager can run reports proving to clients that return on ad spend (ROAS) has gone up, thanks to her efforts. Even when budget cuts come, she'll be tough to fire.

NINE COUNTERINTUITIVE MOVES
FOR LIFE-CHANGING FREELANCE INCOME

An e-commerce consultant like my friend Andy is closer to the money than a brand consultant. He identifies strategic and tactical website changes and works with his team to implement them. Later, he can use metrics, such as cart conversions and average order value (AOV), to draw a clear line of attribution between those changes and revenue growth.

Here are three other examples from freelancers with three different skill sets:

- Adrienne Johnston built a $200,000 per year business designing presentations and pitch decks. Pitch decks are closer to the money than visual identity or editorial design.

- Jake Milner of Nercher Consulting landed a consulting retainer (twelve months at $13,750 per month) with a light manufacturing company. Using their data, Jake helped his client figure out exactly how much material to order and when to order it. The manufacturer was able to avoid tying up too much of their cash in surplus inventory. Jake's mix of analysis, financial controls, and ordering strategy is closer to the money than the high-level consulting most CPAs do to minimize a company's tax liability.

- Joel Klettke is a conversion copywriter and the founder of Case Study Buddy, which offers case studies as a productized service. Individual case study assets start at $4,000, and packages range from $5,000 to $15,000 plus. Those prices look like a bargain when Case Study Buddy's own case studies include past clients like Chris

Dreyer of Rankings.io, who was pleased with the return on investment: "We've closed $179,444 worth of deals in the past month and case studies helped close them all."[1] According to Joel, "Companies will pay a premium for [a well-written case study] because it's tougher to do."[2] Sales assets like case studies are closer to the money than web copywriting.

How close are you and your current offers to the money? How can you create a stronger correlation between the services you provide and the dollars-and-cents outcomes your clients want?

Sometimes, determining the value can be as simple as following up with past clients and asking what happened after you delivered the project. You'd need to do this to write a strong case study anyway.

As you track both your effective hourly rate for various projects and positive outcomes for clients, you can double down on the specific packages or offers that will pay well and be easier to sell.

Bank on Variability in Earning and Volatility in Spending

Imagine that your feet could grow and shrink independently. One night, both feet are the same size. The next morning, your right foot has tripled in size to circus clown proportions.

Our earning and spending are those bewitched, mismatched feet. Countless factors can cause either to expand or contract,

NINE COUNTERINTUITIVE MOVES
FOR LIFE-CHANGING FREELANCE INCOME

independently. A single text message can drain your emergency fund: "Dad's in the hospital. Can you fly home tonight?"

The need for more money can also be quite predictable and manageable. Reasons for spending more can be temporary, such as saving for a once-in-a-lifetime trip to Iceland or buying an engagement ring, and they can be permanent, not to mention quite loud, hungry, and poopy: "We just had a baby."

No matter how painstaking your planning is or how careful your calculations, variability in your earning and volatility in your spending come with the freelance territory. You may end up losing income you were counting on precisely when you needed more of it.

One of my coaching clients sent me this message on a Thursday: "Been a tough week here—lost two clients out of the blue. Taking ten deep breaths and trying to see this as an opportunity."

An early client of mine once told me after I had already finished a project that she was "canceling" it. I could keep the project deposit, she said, but she wasn't going to pay the project balance. Say what?! I definitely didn't see that coming, especially from someone I had counted as a friend.

The only predictable thing in freelance (and life and cliché metaphors) is curveballs. The only predictable solution, if you want to call it that, is three pieces of advice that we can more accurately call aspirations:

- Save aggressively. Scrape and scrimp until you've got at least one month's worth of living expenses saved in an emergency or rainy-day fund. These cash reserves represent your Walkaway Power. The best negotiators don't need the deal, and if you know you'll be okay without that potential client who's already making you uneasy, you'll make more strategic decisions your future self will thank you for.

- Always be marketing. Never spend less than thirty minutes a day on marketing and prospecting. Never. You could convince yourself that you're too busy for it, but you'd be wrong. You could convince yourself there won't be consequences down the road, but you'd be wrong. Take it from a recovering self-deceiver: you can't afford to let your pipeline go dry. Give marketing its rightful place at the top of your daily to-do list, and you'll find a way to fit your current client obligations into the time left over. Tell yourself you'll get back to marketing next week or next month, and you'll be serving up your own regret, ice cold.

- Optimize for less billable work each week. Keep fiddling with your prices and offers until you're able to make what you need in twenty to twenty-five billable hours every week. Ratchet up your effective hourly rate bit by bit until you can literally afford to spend only half your work week on client work and the rest on marketing, admin, and being the best boss you've ever had.

Believe what Harvey S. Firestone, the founder of the Firestone Tire and Rubber Company, wrote back in 1926: "Having a surplus is the greatest aid to business judgment that I know—and

I bitterly know what I'm talking about, for I went through years of upbuilding without being able to accumulate a surplus."[3]

Focus On Controllables

You may have stumbled across what is commonly known as the "Serenity Prayer," attributed to American theologian Reinhold Niebuhr. The earliest published version came from Winnifred Crane Wygal, who studied with Niebuhr, in 1933: "God, grant me the serenity to accept the things I cannot change, courage to change the things I can, and wisdom to know the difference."

Some things freelancers can change and control. Some things we can't. Much of our serenity (and sanity) lies in discerning the difference.

- You can control how you vet clients, but you can't control whether they will continue to be fair, reasonable, and respectful for the duration of the project.

- You can control whether your personal budget and business operating budgets are up to date. You can control whether your freelance prices cover your immediate needs and move you toward your long-term goals. You can't control when unforeseen circumstances cause your spending to scream out of sight like a bottle rocket.

My family's spending spiraled out of control in 2022 when we bought a house built in 1941. It turns out that what people call "character" or "charm" in an old house really means "lots of things may break all at once." Splendid.

I couldn't control the dishonest electrician, having to pay the movers twice, the HVAC unit going out within two weeks, the dishwasher we repaired but had to replace anyway, or the old cast-iron pipes and Orangeburg sewer main that constantly backed up.

What I could was my own reactions to those events. I had a choice to grumble about our situation and gnash my teeth at the onslaught of repairs and replacements or hire people to make the fixes and calmly figure out how to finance them all. (I'm imperfect so there was a bit of both.)

We waste significant heartache and headache when we try to hold on to things that are inherently uncontrollable. (Of course, we do! What could be more human?)

As you test your new freelance price, remember to focus on the controllables:

- Clarity around immediate needs: What do you need to earn in gross revenue each month to pay your personal expenses, business operating expenses, and taxes and not go into debt?

- Clarity around long-term goals: If you were to earn a surplus, what would you spend it on? What is the extra income for?

- Up-to-date budget: How will you know when you're making progress on financial long-term goals?

NINE COUNTERINTUITIVE MOVES
FOR LIFE-CHANGING FREELANCE INCOME

What's your plan for your monthly business and personal spending?

You can't perfectly control your spending or earning. Those bewitched feet will trip you up sometimes. What's your plan?

You also can't control how a new prospect responds to your prices.

I once had a call with a CrossFit trainer who told me that a sales deck would be worth $100,000 to the company if they landed only one new account with it. I gave him a couple of packages and prices for the strategy and copywriting—$2,275 and $4,125.

His response showed me that he was more focused on the price than on value: "The main hold up will be the price tag. Just to be transparent, it seems inflated, when the artwork and heavy lifting will come from us."

I knew that my price was reasonable based on my research into what various agencies were charging—$5,000, $6,500, and $9,750. They had longer timelines too!

Knowing that, however, wasn't likely to change his price-conscious paradigm, no matter how many examples of more expensive "competitors" I shared. I stopped pursuing the opportunity.

If you keep a bottle rocket in a clenched fist, you get burned. Serenity says open your hand and receive the lesson, not the blister.

(Please note: Extended metaphors will continue until morale improves.)

Charge Like a Full-Timer Even If You're Not

If you don't depend on freelance income for all your bills, you really can charge less. It's true. Maybe your full-time job has you covered, or you can count on your partner's income. A constant need to generate the next invoice doesn't drive your freelance pricing.

That's fantastic, but I still recommend you proceed through the pricing calculations as though you are a full-time freelancer who cannot afford a more casual, cavalier approach to pricing.

This full-time pricing approach benefits you in three ways:

1. One day soon, you may realize that your financial needs have changed and that you need to update your budget and prices accordingly. Score! You're already set.

2. Your rates will already be smart and sustainable, should you decide to take the full-time freelance plunge in the future.

3. Charging higher prices like a full-time freelancer will help you attract value-conscious clients, which will in turn lead to more fulfilling projects and relationships.

Think about a Timex watch versus a Rolex. A $40 Timex Ironman with a digital movement keeps better time than a $9,000 Rolex Submariner with a mechanical, self-winding movement. The Ironman is more accurate, or functionally superior, as a timekeeping advice, yet the Submariner costs 225 times more and commands more respect.

Why? People perceive more expensive projects and services as having higher value.

We show more respect to expensive things.

Whether or not you agree that people *should* act this way, we do, and smart freelancers use this quirk of human psychology to our advantage.

Whether you're a full-time freelancer flying solo or a part-time freelancer in a two-income household, what you're after is the right prices. The right prices signal value, expertise, and confidence. They strengthen your positioning. They reward you for doing your best work. They are both exciting and sustainable because they cover both your immediate needs and long-term goals.

Clients Buy Outcomes, Not Time

To win at this freelancing game, we need to rethink what we sell and what clients buy from us. Time is not what freelance clients really want or need from us, though that doesn't stop them from asking.

Most freelancers receive emails with lines like this one I got from an agency owner: "I'd love to pay you for a little bit of your time to talk through some stuff on this topic." He wasn't being sly, and he wasn't trying to devalue my expertise by paying me an hourly rate. He simply defaulted to the way many people ask for access to a freelancer's skills or expertise.

Be that as it may, imagine asking a heart surgeon, "Can I buy some of your time?"

When my dad had open heart surgery, he wasn't paying for time in the OR, but for the surgeon's minimum of fifteen years of education and training:

- Four years of undergraduate studies
- Four years of medical school
- Five years of general surgery residency
- Two to three years of specialized cardiac fellowship

Whether the operation took the surgeon ten minutes or ten hours was beside the point. My dad didn't give a mountain of moldy beans about the surgeon's *time*.

My dad, the patient lying on the table, was paying for an outcome: extending his life. That outcome required the surgeon's knowledge of anatomy and medical procedure, expertise and technique in specific surgical operations, judgment and decision-making, and hand-eye coordination and muscle memory—all accumulated over the course of the many, hopefully successful operations that preceded his.

Though I never saw the final bill, I can tell you the price was worth it. My dad would say the same. He's still with us.

Now, let's say I had a pile of rocks at my house that I want to relocate. Thousands of unskilled laborers in the greater Knoxville area could perform the task. There was a pile over here, and now

NINE COUNTERINTUITIVE MOVES
FOR LIFE-CHANGING FREELANCE INCOME

it's over there. I'm still paying for an outcome, but hauling rocks requires no special talent, training, or tools.

Freelancers have much more in common with surgeons than rock haulers. We often solve painful, expensive problems, and the value of the outcome often far exceeds the market rate for an hour of our time.

Take my coaching client Kate, for example. Even for seemingly simple or "easy" tasks, a client can't separate Kate's time from who she is. The client gets the whole package, including Kate's specialized knowledge, creative skills, soft skills, and character and personality traits:

- Kate earned her BA in Public Relations and graduated Summa Cum Laude.

- At her first job out of college with a tech company, she wrote e-books, campaign mailers, blog posts, social media updates and press releases.

- She also got her feet wet with sales, specifically top-funnel lead generation through cold calls and cold emails.

- Kate later coordinated communications for a tourism board, served as a staff writer, and planned and executed group press tours, media visits, and trips to meet with travel editors and freelancers.

- She worked at a PR agency where she oversaw client accounts, created their campaigns, and implemented those campaigns.

When a client asks Kate, "What's your hourly rate?" or "What do you charge?" they don't want her time. They want access to her multi-faceted brilliance, and they're trying to figure out if they can afford to hire her.

The next time you find yourself on the receiving end of either of those questions, respond with a question of your own: "That depends. What would you like to see happen?"

Those nine words shift the client's focus away from your time and toward their desired outcome. Though you won't be performing a quadruple bypass and saving a life, you will often help the client solve a painful, expensive problem. The absence of that problem is worth far more than whatever dollar amount they would assign to your time. Sell outcomes, not hours.

A story about Nikola Tesla will tie a bow on this lesson. Business legend has it that Henry Ford invited Nikola Tesla to his factory to help him solve a problem. Telsa quickly found the source of the problem and drew an X on a boilerplate.

Later, when Ford received an invoice for $10,000, he was taken aback. He asked for an explanation. Tesla sent a second invoice, now itemized:

- $1 for marking the X.
- $9,999 for knowing where to put it.

Is this fact or fable? I don't think it matters. The lesson still applies: What we know is just as valuable as what we do. Combining the two at the right time for the right client can be lucrative. Clients are paying you to solve problems; the amount of time it takes you is irrelevant.

The surgeon, Kate, Nikola Tesla, and you all have the same retort to a time-fixated client, "Oh, you wouldn't be paying for the time I spent solving the problem. You'd be paying for the fifteen years it took to learn how to do it."

Heroism Is a Bad Business Model

You may know the parable about the person who finds a bunch of starfish washed up on the beach and throws one back into the ocean. A bystander points out that the do-gooder can't possibly save them all. The do-gooder replies, "You're right, but I can save one. Doesn't that make all the difference to it?"

"Do what good you can" is a reminder we all need. Meanwhile, let me point out that our clients are not echinoderms doomed until we come to their aid. Our clients are adults with volition, intelligence, and problem-solving capacity. Responsibility for their problems falls on them, not you.

Where the ultimate responsibility lies is crucial to remember when a potential client reaches out with a last-minute project, sob story, or both.

Allow me to set the scene. You guide a prospect through the discovery and proposal phases. You pin a reasonable price on the project. The client balks at it. They harp on how they really need your help, and they really want to work with you, not some flea-bitten freelancer living in a van by the river. Could you possibly maybe help them out on price? They can scrape together $17 cash, a $23.37 Amazon gift card, and two sticks of spearmint gum.

A sob story often accompanies the shoestring budget. Turns out, this project will honor the legacy of Ichabod who died in a horrific basket weaving accident.

Hyperbole aside, the challenge is discerning whether you're talking to genuinely decent people advocating for a worthy cause or someone pulling on your heartstrings to get a discount or fast turnaround.

Early in my freelance career, my insecurity and a genuine desire to serve others caused me to throw my glasses aside, tear off my shirt, and tie on my cape: "You're in a tight spot? I'll save you!"

Sometimes, the project went well and the client gushed praise. Sometimes, it didn't, and a pattern emerged. Clients who had emergencies kept having emergencies. They kept blaming circumstances while I caught glimpses of poor planning, broken process, and office politics. Swooping in and saving the day made me feel good, but freelance heroism didn't address the deeper problems.

I inadvertently trained clients to expect last-minute availability from me. I was enabling and encouraging bad behavior while creating more stress for myself. One client always ended up paying my expedite fees four out of every five projects because they were always running behind their own deadlines. Thanks to them, I coined a term: "institutionalized mediocrity."

Instead of being a hero, be a shrewd freelancer. Notice patterns. Approach with caution those situations highly likely to disrupt your workflow, cause stress, and not pay you an exciting premium for your trouble:

- Every so often, there's simply no avoiding a tight turnaround. You help save a loyal client's derriere. They acknowledge and deeply appreciate you coming to the rescue. They make it up to you one day.

- However, someone else's poor planning doesn't constitute your emergency. Last-minute projects force us to short-circuit our own expertise, abbreviate our proven processes, or blow them up altogether.

- An initial discovery conversation isn't your implicit agreement to help a client navigate their budget constraints. You have no obligation to find a way to make the project "work" because a client feels desperate. The client's budget isn't your problem to solve. Their urgency isn't either.

- If a prospect can't afford what is a reasonable price for you and won't agree to shrink the scope to match their budget, then the project isn't a good fit for you. Bad-fit projects cause blisters.

- When you find yourself being swayed by a sob story—"Oh Ichabod, how we miss thee!"—ask yourself, "Would I have sought out this opportunity because I care deeply about this cause? Or is this person charismatic or persuasive?" Their passion and need does not constitute your call. Take a pass on the project. Take some advice from Derek Sivers: "If you feel anything less than "hell yeah!" about something, say no."[4]

Freelancers must use our headstrings alongside our heartstrings.

Pricing Is Always Fluid

Your fee will seem reasonable one week to the owners of Darling Donut Shop, and the next week, the same amount of work at the same price point will offend the marketing director at Boring Soulless Corporation.

Pricing is always fluid. Always.

No one says you must charge everyone the same price, and if someone does challenge your price, you can point to the many variables and extenuating circumstances that determine what makes a price reasonable for you, or why you may charge more:

- Client's experience working with agencies or freelancers
- Cost of client's problems and/or missed opportunities
- Your specialized knowledge or domain expertise
- Your financial situation and goals
- Your positioning and packaging
- Value of outcome for client
- Your results or reputation
- Client's level of urgency

NINE COUNTERINTUITIVE MOVES
FOR LIFE-CHANGING FREELANCE INCOME

- Project deliverables
- Client's personality
- Your cost of living
- Your confidence
- Project timeline
- Client's industry
- Your skill level
- Client's budget
- Client's goals
- Your brand

Other variables can multiply the time and effort required to finish a project:

- Miscommunication and misunderstandings
- Client's indecisiveness or disorganization
- Client's inefficient or broken processes
- Your inefficient or broken processes
- Extra revisions or changes
- Extra meetings and calls
- Poor time management
- Decision by committee

- Scope creep
- Delays

Freelancing is predictably unpredictable. I started a website project for a financial advisor whose mother died right as we finished the discovery phase. Another time, a coaching client's father ended up in the hospital, and in less than twenty-four hours, she had little time for anything but caring for him. Rightfully so!

At the end of 2018, two presidents of two companies got fired within weeks of one another. The work I was doing with them ground to a halt, and my billing did, too.

Even if you're adept at positioning, packaging, negotiation, and project management, you cannot exert perfect control over any project.

Be kind to yourself. Try not to beat yourself up when a project bombs or your effective hourly rate swirls down the toilet. Extract what insights you can, and reference them when you're pricing the next project:

- How confident are you in your estimate of the time required to deliver a positive outcome?
- How confident are you in the client's ability to stay focused, give helpful feedback, and make timely decisions?
- What if the timeline doubles or triples, or what if the decision-makers or team members change?

Let your pessimism, not optimism, dictate your prices.

Pushback on Price Reveals a Fit or Belief Problem

Some people have that "it can't hurt to ask" mentality. You probably have friends and family who will haggle every chance they can get: How about an appetizer on the house? How about you throw in a hat for free? How about a complimentary upgrade to a suite? Nudge nudge, wink wink.

Though pushing back on price is any prospect's prerogative, what you want is clients with higher lifetime value. You build a profitable, sustainable, satisfying business with value-conscious clients, not penny pinchers. The latter take a toll on your patience and enthusiasm.

Besides, winning a loyal, value-focused client who keeps giving you projects and who pays whatever price you quote takes the same amount of effort as winning one who works every angle to bring your price down.

The trick is identifying what sort of client you're dealing with. Clients who push back on price go into three buckets:

1. Those shopping for a commodity
2. Those fond of negotiating
3. Those short on budget

I'll explain the root issue with each—paradigm, personality, and budget—and give you an effective tactic for differentiating between the second and third.

Clients Shopping for a Commodity

Some prospects have told me my prices were too high because they believed what they were saying. They believed that copywriting or brand development projects had fixed prices, and if my price fell outside whatever range they deemed reasonable, they asked me why they should they pay me more.

They were making an apples-to-apples comparison. In their eyes, I was a commodity in a market of distinguishable options. Comparing the value of a brilliant, seasoned writer's work to a bumbling rookie's would be like comparing an Italian white truffle to a Red Delicious apple, yet price-conscious clients make that mistake all the time.

The challenge here is the price-conscious client's implicit belief that an outcome like a beautiful new e-commerce website "should" cost an amount he considers "reasonable."

Perhaps the gym owner who paid $100 for his first lumpy logo doesn't understand the difference between it and a complete, cohesive identity system. What for him seems like a "fair" price wouldn't cover the kickoff call with an award-winning identity designer, one whose friends think he's undercharging when he goes below $30,000.

What governing body or industry association is the client using to judge such "fairness"? No such measuring stick exists for most freelance disciplines in most industries in most countries. Freelancing is a wildly free market in that respect.

This reality doesn't stop commodity shoppers from treating feeling as fact. Paradigms are donkeys. They're difficult to budge.

You're not going to change a commodity shopper's paradigm in one conversation or ten. You see a truffle. They see an apple. They will insist that you're overcharging and that they can get the same outcome or deliverables elsewhere, for cheaper.

Encourage them to do so.

Clients Fond of Negotiating

Some people pride themselves on never paying full price for anything. It's a personality type. Ever heard of someone driving to a gas station thirty minutes across town to save $0.10 per gallon? Yeah, those people.

The compulsive desire to pay less makes it difficult for them to value their own time or make investments based on long-term value.

Early in my freelance career, I encountered several of these folks. They told me my prices were too high. I believed them. How was I to know any different?

I didn't yet recognize the shape of a negotiation tactic coming into focus: "Let me play ball and see if I can push back on price and get this freelancer to come down."

I did come down a couple of times, usually because they reassured me: "We'll send you lots of work." "This project should be quick and easy." "We'll refer you to everyone." More referrals? Golly, that'd be great!

When the projects didn't prove any easier and the repeat business and referrals never materialized, I realized that I had gotten played. There was nothing wrong with my original price. The client simply wanted to pay less and had, consciously or unconsciously, reached into a bag of negotiation tricks. My inexperience cost me.

The challenge here isn't negotiation itself, which is part of life, but individuals who always ask look for some angle whereby they can extract more value for themselves without giving value in return.

No matter how logical your approach to pricing is and no matter how clearly you quantify the value of the outcomes, you're not going to counteract some people's fixation on playing hardball, even in cases where finding a win-win would align with their self-interest.

Like paradigms, personalities are difficult to change.

Clients Short on Budget

Some prospects told me my prices were too high because they didn't have the budget. They wanted to work with me, and rather than be transparent about their budget constraints, they made my price the issue.

To be clear, many fine people with real budget constraints make fine clients. The last thing I want to do is imply that folks who are short on cash are inept, stingy, or self-centered. As a business owner myself, I understand the cash crunch predicament. I've had five different places I could spend every one dollar. I've had business-class aspirations and a coach bank account. This is the plight of the business owner and creative entrepreneur.

At the same time, I don't want to come down on my freelance prices because I don't want to teach clients that all they need to do to get a discount is balk at the original price. Freelancers don't run charities. We're not grocery stores running a promotion on canned green beans. We don't have a home improvement franchise that accepts competitors' coupons.

We want to approach cash-strapped prospects with empathy while we answer these questions:

- Is the core issue the tight budget or is it the person's paradigm or personality as described above?

- Can a different, smaller project scope effectively address a client need and kickstart the relationship?

Should You Try to Persuade Price-Conscious Prospects?

As I already explained, I don't think there's much you can do with price-conscious prospects. You're deceiving yourself if you think conversations about money will get easier once the client has more cash. Even if you can convince them you're worth what you charge, you'll keep colliding with their must-save-money paradigm.

When you realize a prospect is treating you and your work as a commodity, politely excuse yourself from the conversation. You can certainly keep in touch and hope their urgency increases until they will scrape together a budget, but in my experience, you're better off pursuing and investing in other relationships.

There's always someone who charges less, and as soon as they find a cheaper option, they'll leave. Because there was never going to be any loyalty, the upside for you and your business is negligible.

Should You Try to Negotiate?

A willingness or eagerness to lock horns with prospects signals that you've got the personality for it. My friend Joey has this capability. He treats negotiation like a game of chess, and he can play to win without bruising the relationship.

I'm just not that way. The chess match irritates me, especially when a prospect makes some gripe about the price and doesn't back it up with evidence or logic. Making a claim isn't the same as building a case backed with evidence.

Granted, in some cases, otherwise reasonable people will make unqualified statements like "the price seems inflated" because creativity seems vague and squishy to them. They don't fully grasp the taste, expertise, and process required to produce positive outcomes, and thus the prices for writing, design, or marketing consulting seem arbitrary. They would never try to negotiate a lower price for a meal at a fine-dining restaurant or seat on a plane.

If your prospect seems reasonable, if uninformed, then you can provide a little freelance pricing education couched as a polite, thoughtful response.

Whether you call conversations with clients about money negotiation or education, you must know yourself. Does verbal sparring leave you feeling bruised and drained before the project has even started? Or do you find it energizing?

Seek out clients who align with your personality and values.

I prefer to talk candidly with clients about what they want and how much money they have to spend, and if we can't find a win-win, then I'll be the first to propose that we part ways amicably. I'm not looking to beat anyone, and I've found plenty of clients who share my preferences.

How to Differentiate between Diehard Negotiators and Cash-Strapped Prospects

When either type pushes back on price, clamp down any irritation you feel in the moment and say these words: "I totally understand budget constraints. What would you like to remove from the scope?"

Reasonable people with real budget constraints will recognize that you have no obligation to offer the same amount of work at a price lower than you originally quoted. They will see that you are looking for a reasonable compromise, and it's logical that you'd offer to shrink the scope to match their budget.

Problem solved: They stay within their budget and get some help, albeit a little less than they wanted. You shrink the scope and come down on price without discounting your services and thereby undermining your positioning and expertise.

As for anyone who raises a stink about paying less for a smaller project because you wouldn't give a just-because discount on the bigger one, walk away as quickly as your dignity allows. Smile, too, because you just dodged a bullet.

Maybe It's Your Problem, Not Theirs

Before we move on, I want to tease out two more client types who may push back on price:

1. The prospect who doesn't believe in the project's value. Maybe the marketing director has tried content marketing in the past and been underwhelmed by the results. Maybe the startup founder got burned by the last freelancer she hired and is understandably skeptical of your ability to deliver. It's natural for people to balk at the price when they don't really believe that a transformation is about to occur. Freelancers must be prepared to talk about the return on investment: "twelve more inbound leads from your website per month." Or we must paint a detailed, enticing of the before and after: "you'll finally have the beautifully clear and concise brand messaging that resonates deeply with your dream clients and makes them eager to connect with you." Otherwise, why would even value-focused prospects set aside their skepticism?

2. The prospect who doesn't believe you're an expert. This is the hardest horse pill to swallow. You may be one of the top authorities in your specialization—for example, helping grow software as a service (SaaS) companies through clever affiliate programs. You may be able to start campfires with your mind and crush foes a sweep of

NINE COUNTERINTUITIVE MOVES
FOR LIFE-CHANGING FREELANCE INCOME

your arm. But if your reputation doesn't precede you, if you don't have that positioning and perceived authority out in the market, then even respectful, value-conscious clients will be reluctant to pay what you truly deserve.

When someone isn't willing to pay what you ask, they're not challenging or discounting your innate value. They're expressing a disconnect between your price and their perception of the project's value.

To change a client's perception of a "fair" price, you must change what they believe about the value.

Belief precedes premium fees, and Alex Hormozi says that the sales process is a vehicle for belief: "Selling is a transference of belief over a bridge of trust. Therefore you cannot sell unless you believe. And they will not buy unless they believe YOU."[5]

If I asked you to give me $10 in exchange for $20, would you agree? Of course. You believe that you can double your money with zero effort.

What if I offered to take away your lower back pain and had dozens of testimonials from happy clients to back up my claims? Would you pay me a significant amount of money to improve your quality of life? Yes.

Before you can reasonably expect to consistently charge at or above your Dream Rate, you need strong positioning and proof of your authority and ability to deliver.

You also need a strategic, structured discovery and proposal process—aka, sales process—that enables the client's belief in you to walk over the bridge. That way, their generous budget can follow.

Projects That Pay the Most Don't Always Pay the Best

Back in 2016 I had a breakthrough with my freelance pricing. At the time I was COO of Closeup.fm, a tech startup I had invested $25,000 in and co-founded. Closeup consumed 75 percent of my time and paid 0 percent of my bills. Startups are so cool until you're too tired to care.

I was burning down fast, and as sole breadwinner for my family, I felt a wee bit of pressure to, you know, come up with chicken nuggets and carrots for my wife and two kids. I needed to make more money, but as I poked at the various projects I'd recently sold, I realized that projects with higher prices don't always pay the best.

Whether you charge by the hour or project, you spend a certain amount of time completing that project. When you divide the final fee by the time spent, you get an effective hourly rate (EHR).

In 2016 I was charging around $500 for a page of web copy (up to 500 words) and $750 for a blog post (up to 1,000 words).

The blog post paid more. Any smart freelancer would try to sell more blog posts, right? Wrong.

NINE COUNTERINTUITIVE MOVES
FOR LIFE-CHANGING FREELANCE INCOME

Because I'd tracked my time, I knew the approximate EHR for both web copy and blog content projects.

- An efficient process built around questionnaires and templates enabled me to knock out a page of web copy in around 2.5 hours. $500 divided by 2.5 gave me an EHR of $200.

- A blog post took me 4.25 hours. $750 divided by 4.25 gave me an EHR of $176.47.

The difference between $176.47 and $200 may look small, but that extra 12 percent took on more significance when I applied the math to many projects over a year. Twenty-nine blog posts would have taken me around 125 hours to finish and brought in $21,750. With that same 125 hours, I could have written fifty pages of web copy and made $25,000.

A page of web copy had a lower price but a higher EHR, and an extra $3,250 over a year symbolized several months' worth of nuggets and carrots.

Don't let initial price fool you. Projects that pay the most don't always pay the best. Your biggest money isn't always your best money.

My most strategic growth came once I identified, marketed, and sold productized services with a higher EHR. Perhaps yours will, too.

Creative Projects Don't Have Set Prices

What would you expect to pay for a burger under a heat lamp at a gas station? What about a burger crafted by chef Alain Ducasse who has three Michelin stars?

Prices aren't static on most things, and creative services least of all.

I once got a spam text about a $9.99 logo, complete with a "100 percent satisfaction and money-back guarantee." Though I doubt that a $10 logo and "satisfaction" go hand in hand, the text proved that prices for creative projects, including logo design, don't have a bottom.

In 2000, BP Amoco raised eyebrows when they paid design firm Landor £136 million to redesign and roll out the company's visual identity.[6] Prices for creative projects don't have an upper limit either.

You can pay $10, $100, $1,000, $10,000, $100,000, or far more for a logo. What can possibly explain such a huge variance?

A story about an entrepreneur and a designer offers insight. After resigning from Apple in May 1985, Steve Jobs founded NeXT, Inc., and he needed a corporate identity for the new venture.

An employee gave Jobs several books and articles by modernist designer Paul Rand. Rand had already created identities for some of the most iconic brands of his era, including Ford, UPS, ABC, IBM, and Westinghouse.

NINE COUNTERINTUITIVE MOVES
FOR LIFE-CHANGING FREELANCE INCOME

When Jobs approached Rand about the project in 1986, he told Jobs that the project would cost $100,000, or around $250,000 at today's value. Steve Jobs described Rand's rather blunt approach in an interview in 1993: "I asked him [Paul Rand] if he would come up with a few options, and he said, 'No, I will solve your problem for you. And you will pay me.'"[7]

Was Paul Rand's work quantifiably a hundred times better than every contemporary who charged $1,000? No.

Sheer talent or skill doesn't explain Rand's price.

Like copywriting, code, and hamburgers, identity design has no fixed price.

A project is worth what a client is willing to pay. What a client will pay goes up with perceived value. Perceived value goes up with perceived authority, context, and the "packaging" of the offer.

Rand was a recognized authority. He had the guts to name that price. He had the confidence that he could deliver. Swagger matters, and clearly, he convinced Jobs. Jobs paid Rand's fee, and decades later, you're hearing the story.

Here's an uncomfortable insight: freelancers often blame clients for our woes, yet we set our own prices.

Our prices attract a certain type of client, either ones we want or ones we don't, and our authority, guts, and confidence ultimately determine what we're able to charge. Whether those of us obsessed with craft and quality like it or not, freelancers with B-grade work who understand their target audience's pains and problems, who nail their positioning and messaging, and who craft juicy offers will flourish while their peers with more talent or better quality and outcomes flounder.

Maybe you weren't born in New York City like Rand. Maybe you didn't attend Parsons School of Design. Maybe you don't have the nerve to quote an astronomical fee—yet.

Focus on the advantages you do have or can acquire. Reassess your self-imposed psychological barriers and your niche:

- What if you knew that shifting to a particular pricing strategy would reinforce your expertise and help you stand out from competitors?

- What if you were confident that your freelance pricing was sending the right signals about your brand, services, and value?

- What if you were to pivot to a different niche that places a higher value on the outcomes you deliver?

Without a doubt, the quality of our work product certainly helps perceived authority. Paul Rand's work was truly iconic.

However, Rand still had to put in the work. His father didn't believe he could make a living with art, and Rand was mostly self-taught. One of his first jobs was creating stock images for newspapers and magazines. Nothing to write home about. In exchange for full artistic freedom, he had designed covers for *Direction* magazine for no fee.

NINE COUNTERINTUITIVE MOVES FOR LIFE-CHANGING FREELANCE INCOME

That's right, he broke the cardinal rule of the freelance world—no free work!—and those covers helped to build his international reputation.

Creative projects don't have fixed prices. You can charge whatever you like if clients want what you have badly enough. The question is, does your reputation precede you? Does it give you leverage?

If not, what are you going to do about that?

We must embrace the subtler, harder work of strong positioning: clear, concise messaging around your target audience's problems, needs, and goals; packaging your services as juicy offers; making clients feel seen and understood; and standing your ground when a client's vision for the project or workflow poses a threat to the very outcomes they're paying you to deliver.

There's Always Someone Who Charges Less

In a competitive marketplace there's always someone who will sell a project for a stupid, unsustainable price. Or for free! (I'm looking at you, Paul Rand.)

Remember that text message I got with the $9.99 logo offer? Yeah, certain folks play pricing limbo ("How low can you go, how low can you go!") and turn freelancing into a race to the bottom.

Smart freelancers bow out of that race. We don't try to compete based on price. We don't try to make ourselves a "good deal."

And we certainly don't let our own budget constraints lead us to believe that every potential client's top priority is saving money. What represents a significant sum for you may be a small line item for a value-conscious client.

Many things may be more important to them than getting a lower price:

- Working with a subject matter expert who won't have a learning curve

- Working with a known authority with a proven track record

- Achieving a very specific result in a predictable timeframe

- Getting it done faster with minimal oversight required

- Avoiding delays, embarrassment, and hassles

- Clear, copious, consistent communication

- Client education / training / resources

- Personal responsibility for mistakes

- Specialization / domain expertise

- Promises kept and deadlines met

- Creating clarity and confidence

- Effective project management

- Memorable client experience

NINE COUNTERINTUITIVE MOVES FOR LIFE-CHANGING FREELANCE INCOME

- Your network / relationships
- Easier or better packaging
- Personality and humor
- Long-term value
- Mitigation of risk
- Better strategy
- Proven process
- High quality
- Leadership
- Simplicity
- Fun

Your competitors are going to do whatever they're going to do. Ignore their prices, and the rest of the freelance market doing the funky chicken dance on stilts on ice. It's crazy and unsustainable, and someone's going to get hurt.

But not you. The true predictors of what you *can* charge are what you believe about money, your reputation or authority, the right niche, having the swagger to name the price that's right for *you*, and having the gumption to deliver.

Swagger matters more than "the competition," my friends. Your job isn't to be competitive with your prices, but to charge commensurate to the value you create, without lowering prices or piling on more stuff.

To get the audacious project fee, you must ask for it. Your clients aren't going to wake up one day, and say, "You know, I really ought to pay her more."

Freelancing Isn't a Meritocracy

In my graduate creative writing program, the last labels an aspiring man of letters wanted slapped on his work were "derivative," "predictable," or "plainspoken." Formulaic writing—think: an Agatha Christie plot—was met with disdain. We were all chasing originality, and when a fellow poet told me one of my poems was "too romantic," I questioned my life choices for weeks.

Herman Melville once wrote in an article of literary criticism that "It is better to fail in originality, than to succeed in imitation."[8] Who was I to disagree?

When I entered the world of freelancing, I couldn't help but bring the trappings and fixations of the literary world with me. I considered myself an artist. I wanted to produce art. I was in for a shock.

Freelancing isn't a meritocracy. The most talented freelancers don't always win the project or stay in business. From a client's standpoint, superior outcomes often don't require originality or superior quality in the creative or work product.

One specific memory from my six-month stint at a marketing agency comes to mind. I was tasked with writing some copy for a local sushi restaurant and felt quite proud of one billboard headline: "Sushi Couture."

NINE COUNTERINTUITIVE MOVES
FOR LIFE-CHANGING FREELANCE INCOME

When I shared my idea with the creative director, he asked me what "couture" meant.

"You know, 'couture' as in high fashion and bespoke garments?" I said. "What sushi lover wouldn't love that attention to detail in their rolls and nigiri!"

"We can't use that," he said. "No one in East Tennessee will know what that means."

That stopped me in my tracks. Clearly, the creative director hadn't read the Melville article, but could I disagree with him?

I didn't know much about marketing and advertising yet, but I did understand that the purpose of a billboard is to build brand awareness through repeated exposure, not to demonstrate some nobody copywriter's cleverness or wide vocabulary.

"Couture" couldn't hold a candle to "Yo, driver! Local restaurant. Nama. Good sushi."

Freelancers can succeed at being original or clever yet still fail at the business objective, which in this case meant getting a key differentiator across clearly in three seconds.

The economics and measures of effectiveness in freelancing are different from the world of art and literature. You're not trying to win a Pulitzer, Nobel Prize, or Guggenheim Fellowship. Even winning Addys, Golden Lions, and other industry awards doesn't guarantee you'll thrive long term.

This reality doesn't stop freelancers from trying to correlate talent and financial success. The narrative goes something like this: "If I just keep my head and do good work, everything will work out all right in the end."

Will it? Are talent, good work, or quality the only red bricks you need to build a thriving freelance business?

Who arbitrates what "quality" is, the freelancer or the client? And is "good" work the only kind that is effective from the client's perspective? Could you find a stunningly original visual identity for a tech startup that in no way connects with their target audience? Sure. And could you find dozens of WordPress websites with rotten code generating beaucoup leads? Sure.

As much as the craftsman in me would love to believe that creative talent, like love, is all we need, the pragmatist in me can't ignore the evidence.

Art and commerce do mix, but good art isn't enough to woo good commerce. We must proactively acquire the skills on the commerce side. Your artistic or creative talent must work in tandem with your marketing, pricing, fulfillment, and spending talent. Remove a tire, and the freelance go-kart veers straight into a tree.

Even if your creative skills are quantifiably better, higher, and more ethereal than a million Monarch butterflies, you can miss out on the clients you want if you fail to mention what they want. You tout your "award-winning" this or "top-quality" that while they're thinking, "Yeah, I just need someone who can deliver on time." Predictability, convenience, speed, efficiency, the mitigation of risk, and "acceptable" quality motivate them more than superior quality.

NINE COUNTERINTUITIVE MOVES
FOR LIFE-CHANGING FREELANCE INCOME

Ironically, high quality can keep freelancers stuck the same as low prices.

Freelancing isn't a meritocracy. Quality gives you one advantage in a sea of mediocrity, but you need others to thrive long term: positioning, packaging, pricing, specialization, process, consistent marketing, mindset, and recognized authority.

Remember:

- Better questions lead to better insights, and better insights lead to bigger proposals.

- Get closer to the money if you can. You'll find it to charge based on the value you create.

- Bank on variability in earning and volatility in spending. Save aggressively until you have a surplus. A surplus improves your judgment and gives you walkaway power.

- Focus on what you can change and control, not what you can't. Much of our serenity and sanity comes from knowing the difference between the two.

- Charge like a full-time freelancer even if you're not.

- Sell outcomes, not hours.

- Heroism is a bad business model. Notice patterns, and approach with cautions those situations that are highly likely to disrupt your workflow, cause stress, and not pay you an exciting premium for your trouble.

- Pricing is always fluid. No one says you must charge everyone the same price. Many variables and extenuating circumstances determine what makes a price reasonable for you. Let your pessimism, not optimism, dictate your prices.

- Pushback on price reveals a fit or belief problem. The root issue may be the client's paradigm, personality, or budget. To change a client's perception of a "fair" price, you must change what they believe about the value. Clients will not buy unless they believe in you.

- Projects that pay the most don't always pay the best. Your biggest money isn't always your best money. Your most strategic growth will come from productized services with higher EHR.

- Creative projects don't have fixed prices. A project is worth what a client is willing to pay. What a client will pay goes up with perceived value. Perceived value goes up with perceived authority, context, and the "packaging" of the offer.

- There's always someone who charges less. Bow out of the race to the bottom.

- Freelancing isn't a meritocracy. Even if your creative skills are quantifiably better, you can miss out on the clients you want because you fail to mention what they want. Quality gives you one advantage, but you need others to thrive long term.

See you in Move Eight.

NINE COUNTERINTUITIVE MOVES FOR LIFE-CHANGING FREELANCE INCOME

These vitamins won't do you much good if you often forget to take them. I created a convenient cheat sheet to help you remember. Go to austinlchurch.com/free-money-resources to download it for free. Enjoy.

MOVE EIGHT:

◇◇◇◇◇◇◇◇◇◇◇

Get Answers

THE PREVIOUS CHAPTER COVERED VITAMINS YOU SHOULD TAKE—THE LESSONS, PRINCIPLES, AND BEST PRACTICES THAT COMPLEMENT THE PRICING PROCESS IN THE FIRST PART OF THE BOOK. Setting smart, strategic prices is one thing, and getting those prices is another.

This chapter contains answers to some of the questions freelancers ask me most often. Save yourself headaches and heartache by scanning them to see if any are top of mind for you.

Is there ever a time when billing hourly is the right move?

Yes. Charging hourly minimizes risk in several situations.

If you're relatively new to freelancing, you may still be figuring out how long certain tasks and projects take. What if you plan for five hours and the project takes you ten? You would effectively cut your hourly rate in half. Charging a flat fee can be risky until you nail down your process and estimates.

NINE COUNTERINTUITIVE MOVES
FOR LIFE-CHANGING FREELANCE INCOME

The hourly model can also protect you from clients who have a history of blowing scope. One content producer named Cat worked full-time for a company for five years. After she left, her last employer became her first freelance client. Long experience had taught Cat that projects would balloon, and any flat fee that she quoted would come back to bite her. Cat did enjoy the team and the work itself, and the extra work wasn't an issue if she charged hourly.

As Cat discovered, the easiest way to account for messes and moving targets is to charge hourly. Freelance cleanup on aisle nine! You sacrifice some upside to make your life easier, but that may be worth it to you, assuming the client is reasonable and self-aware, if a bit scattered and disorganized.

Hourly can also simplify your life in situations where the client has a punch list of smaller needs or deliverables, some of which may be hard to estimate until you're in the middle of them.

Software engineers and designers often find themselves in this situation. Selling a time block of ten or twenty hours as a "minimum engagement" can get a quick yes from the client. You get paid to knock out several straightforward projects and help them figure out how much time is required to knock out the more complex ones. You're one part handyman and one part sleuth.

To be clear, the hourly model penalizes your skill, efficiency, and expertise, but it can be the right tool for minimizing risk based on your level of experience, a specific relationship, or the nature of certain projects.

You can always switch pricing models later.

Which Pricing Model Is Right For Me?

There is no one-size-fits-all pricing "solution" for freelancers. That may be the most important takeaway in this chapter.

Pricing models are neither good nor bad. Each one is simply a tool in your freelance kit. Every freelance and consulting gig has risks, some easy to predict and some hard. You must analyze the client, project, and circumstances and pick the right tool for the job.

The right pricing tool does three things for you:

1. Manages risk
2. Maximizes revenue
3. Strengthens positioning

If you were in the kitchen and had both a watermelon and carrots to cut, you'd be wise to use a chef's knife for the former and a paring knife for the latter. You don't want to cut yourself. The right knife minimizes that risk.

In freelancing the goal isn't to mitigate risk entirely. Some risk can be good because whoever takes the risk gets the upside.

If you charge hourly, you pass the risk and the upside to the client. If the project takes longer than expected or keeps changing her mind, the price goes up. She took the risk, and she paid a higher price. If you do good work quickly, the client pays less for it. She took the risk, and she got the upside by paying a lower price.

If you charge a flat fee, you take the risk. For example, let's say a freelance writer would ordinarily charge $100 an hour and expect to spend ten hours writing a white paper from scratch. But with one client, he decides to charge a flat fee of $1,000 instead. There was the risk that the project would take twelve hours, but it only takes eight. He took the risk and got the upside by making a 25 percent higher effective hourly rate ($125).

Your risk tolerance will fluctuate, based on everything from spending habits and personality to mindset and your mother-in-law's travel schedule. Sometimes, you'll feel audacious enough to throw out a higher number and let the chips fall where they may. Sometimes, you'll think, "I can't be super aggressive with my prices right now. My kid needs braces."

You don't need to beat yourself up or feel like a second-rate freelancer for charging hourly or not relentlessly nudging your prices higher.

Be kind to yourself while recognizing that you'll only be satisfied with your freelance business long term if you charge based on the value you create.

Keep working on an asymmetric relationship between the time you put in and the money you get out. Keep searching for that value-focused pricing sweet spot. Throw out an outrageous price on occasion just to see what happens.

If your prices aren't offending someone, you're undercharging.

Consultant and host of the Ditching Hourly podcast, Jonathan Stark, reminds us that we're optimizing for ideal buyers, not everyone else:

Good pricing always seems outrageous to somebody. All that matters is that your prices are acceptable to your ideal buyers. It doesn't matter what your friends, family, colleagues, strangers on Reddit, or anyone else thinks. If nobody thinks your prices are outrageous, you haven't found your sweet spot yet.[1]

Check out the pricing models in the next section and then decide which one is right for you, right now.

What Are the Most Common Freelance Pricing Models?

These are the seven most common pricing models:

- Hourly
- Fixed Price, Fixed Scope (or, Flat Fee)
- Value-Based
- Retainers (or Monthly Subscriptions)
- Equity for Services
- Fixed Timeframe (or VIP Daily or Weekly Sprints)
- Performance-Based

If you'd like to read a deeper analysis of all seven models, go to the Appendix. There, I break down the pros and cons and share tips for using each model effectively.

How Do You Raise a Price with an Existing Client without Scaring Them Away?

Raise your prices in 10, 15, or 25 percent increments.

Blame inflation, your destructive puppy, or me: "Hey, I was talking to my business coach, Austin, and we determined that I need to raise my prices by 10 percent."

Worth noting: I have never lost a client over a 10 percent price hike. That extra amount hasn't been high enough to motivate a client to leave.

Freelancers forget that replacing us is downright inconvenient. I can attest to that. When the freelance designer had I worked with for years got a full-time job at a New York City agency, I was happy for her and bummed for myself. Finding a new designer was one more thing I had to do.

Assuming that your clients are satisfied, the majority would rather fork over extra money than go through the hassle of hiring someone new.

I've helped a lot of freelancers raise their prices, and what tripped many of them up previously was knowing how to broach the subject with their existing clients. The best approach is a clear, polite, and firm rate increase email.

If you don't have this email written already, go to austinlchurch.com/free-money-resources, and download my rate increase email template for free. Enjoy.

What's a Good Timeline for Raising My Prices?

Short answer: Right now. Isn't that why you read this book?

Longer answer: If you're accumulating more and more credit card debt every single month, then you literally cannot afford to not raise your prices every three to six months (or with every new client) until you've got more stability and sustainability.

If you've got some savings and a longer runway, then you can afford to ratchet up your prices at a more casual pace without a high risk of losing loyal clients.

Stay positive. Some clients will stick with you because they like you, they appreciate the quality of your work, and they know you've been undercharging. They'll think, "Good things can't last forever," and happily pay your higher prices.

What If I Raise My Prices and Lose a Client?

First, turn lemons into a freelance lemonade stand. Losing a client means freeing up time and attention. You will be making *more* from the clients who stick with you, and you can offer the freed-up capacity to them first.

Instead of doubling down on freaking out and feeding your anxiety, kick your marketing into overdrive: "All right, I need to be that much more serious. I have ten hours a month that I'm going to use to replace ACME Corporation ASAP."

Make the math work out in your favor by spending your freed-up capacity on prospecting for higher-paying clients. Go after the clients you really want.

I've got an emergency tool kit of fifteen marketing tactics for getting clients fast. You can reach for it when a client drops you suddenly, or when you reach a breaking point and decide to rehome a client.

Go to austinlchurch.com/free-money-resources to get the tool kit.

How Do You Set Subcontracting Rates?

I believe in paying people what they believe is fair. When I'm talking to subcontractors about money, I default to full transparency: "I want you to be happy. Collaborating should be a satisfying for us both. Tell me what you want to make."

If there's an unbridgeable gulf between their definition of fair and my own, then we're not a good fit. I've had some subcontractors throw out numbers and I've had to respond, "Sorry, I can't afford that."

I made it clear I wasn't negotiating. I simply didn't have the money, and if I didn't have any wiggle room on the scope and they didn't have any wiggle room on their fee, then we wouldn't work together. It really can be that simple, with no intense emotion required.

A fair exchange of value is what we're after with our clients and subcontractors. We want both parties to walk away happy. A line from the 2008 film *The Brothers Bloom* comes to mind:

"The perfect con is one where everyone involved gets just what they wanted."[2]

Sidenote: If you know that a subcontractor is undercharging you, consider paying above their asking price—or Fair Plus. A freelance designer once asked me, "Would you be okay with $30 an hour?" I replied, "No, but I'd be okay with $50 an hour. How does that sound?" She was stunned at first, but it won't surprise you that we have a strong, trusting relationship. She will fit my projects in, even when she's busy.

Fair Plus may take a little cash out of your pocket in the short term, but you'll never regret it in the long term.

How Do You Justify Pricing If a Client Doesn't Think Your Price Is Worth It?

As I mentioned in the vitamins chapter, pushback on price reveals a fit or belief problem. The client wants to play hard ball, or, more often, they don't see the value.

You may have twice the experience of whoever else they're talking to, triple the talent, and ten times the number of client success stories, yet some clients will still struggle to look past the initial price to the eventual return on investment.

Or perhaps they aren't talking to another freelancer, and they don't understand the role that hard-won expertise plays in positive, *valuable* project outcomes. You know they'd be walking circles in the woods without your expert guidance.

Meanwhile, they made an ill-informed guess about what the project "should" cost, and any delta above that, however reasonable from your perspective, would make them say, "No, no, no, that's too high."

You and the client are at an impasse until they tell you what they had in mind. In these situations, my friend Ilise Benun, author of *The Creative Professional's Guide to Money*, reaches for a specific question:

The line that works almost every time, is, 'Are you thinking $500, $5,000 or $50,000?' You see, you and your prospect must be on the same page money-wise in order to decide if you should even price it in the first place. And once you know what they're thinking, which is also how they value the project, you can come up with a price that covers your expenses, includes a profit and often more.

You assign one value to the project. The client assigns another. Clients who don't know better will compress your colorful, three-dimensional expertise, experience, and creative and problem-solving skills into a gray cog that fits somewhere their little business engine.

It's every freelancer's job to show a potential client that you're not an interchangeable part.

Positioning yourself as an expert in each prospect's mind starts long before you've named your price or asked a client to name theirs. Expertise comes through in the messaging on your website, case studies, and the questions you ask in an intake questionnaire. I've also found it helpful to send a welcome deck a day or two before the discovery conversation.

It's safer to assume that any potential client doesn't know your full capabilities. The deck tells a story that makes hiring you highly desirable: who you are, what you do, why it matters, key steps of your process, key outcomes, and proof in the form of endorsements, work samples, succinct case studies, or testimonials.

People want to hire experts. They're certainly willing to pay experts more than novices. Make your expertise obvious and unmistakable throughout your marketing, discovery, and sales process. Illuminate their predicament and enable them to self-diagnose: "I'm lost in the woods."

Later, you won't need to justify your price.

To see several examples of welcome decks, go to austinlchurch.com/free-money-resources.

How Do You Respond When Someone Asks What You Charge?

When a client asks, "What do you charge for [insert project]?" or "What's your hourly rate?" respond with these nine words: "That depends, what would you like to see happen?"

What you or I charge is immaterial until we know whether the client has a project that we can help with and whether the value of the project's outcome justifies our involvement and fees.

Our objective early in the discovery process isn't to give them a price but to help them get clarity, define the challenges and the various paths forward, and define the value of the outcomes.

If you blurt out your rates out of nervousness or habit, you're inviting a comparison to the last freelancer they spoke with or hired, and one who may lack your experience, expertise, and talent.

The better approach is to whip out that nine-word response and shift their attention away from your rates to their problems. Act as a consultant and facilitate a process of self-discovery first. Only once you and the client agree on the root problem, the project or path forward, and the desired outcomes—that is, the scope—do you start estimating your fees.

Do You Charge Retainer Clients Less for One-Off Projects?

Even if a client already pays for a monthly retainer or subscription, I usually don't charge less for one-off projects. I also don't offer new clients a price break even if the retainers I've stacked up already cover my monthly income needs.

If I'm quoting a one-off project or retainer, whether for an existing client or a new one, I always start with the same base unit of calculation—my Dream Rate. Then, I add more cushion on top of that (Pessimistic Pricing) and make the final price weirdly specific.

The crux of the pricing methodology in this book is knowing your Survival Rate and Dream Rate and keeping your sight fixed on the entire year of earning, not the project right in front of you.

Every hour you bill at your Dream Rate or higher adds to the flywheel effect. You're making more money in less time, which frees up more hours to spend on marketing and prospecting, which in turn fills your pipeline with high-quality leads, which enables you to be more selective and work with clients willing to pay fees at or above your Dream Rate.

Charging less for one-off projects creates the opposite effect. You make hitting your Dream Rate across a year more difficult and slow the flywheel.

Can you be generous? Can you make exceptions? Absolutely. Just be cognizant of the tradeoffs and the ripple effect across the year.

If I Offer Services as Packaged "Engagements," How Should I Approach Pricing on My Website?

Use your minimum engagement—for example, "starting at $5,000"—on your Services (or similar) page to set expectations.

You can also add a "budget range" field to your contact form. If your minimum engagement is $5,000, then don't include a $0 to $5,000 option. The first one would be $5,000 to $10,000. That way, you repel people who don't have a big enough budget before they get in touch.

Freelancers have nothing to gain long-term by being the cheap or affordable option. Being "expensive" is good for your positioning, and later, after the discovery conversation, you can shrink the scope to match the budget, as needed.

What Is Value-Based Pricing?

Value-Based pricing involves quantifying the potential value of the outcome for the client and make your fee a fraction of that.

For example, let's say you're a designer and developer who helps coaches, consultants, and creators generate more leads with their websites. One of your prospects tells you that the average lead is worth $1,000.

You would quantify the value like this:

An average lead is worth $1,000, and I can help you get another twenty leads per month. If you close half those leads, that's an extra $10,000 a month, or $120,000 a year. What I propose is a new website and lead generation strategy in two phases: $14,725 for Phase I and $1,675 a month for six months for Phase II. That's $24,775 total to help you generate $120,000 worth of leads.

Quantifying value and setting value-based prices is easier for some freelancers and consultants than others. If the client doesn't know some of their key metrics, such as the average value of a lead, you may have a harder time. Or, if the value is bound up with the emotional benefits, such as pride in a new brand identity and confidence to market the brand more aggressively, you may have a harder time.

If you've already been through the pricing exercises in the first part of this book, then you're familiar with Pessimistic Prices and the benefit of making it weirdly precise. Value-based pricing can mean anything above your weirdly precise price.

If you listen closely, potential clients will always tell you what they want to buy and how they want you to sell it to them. Better questions lead to better insights, and better insights lead to bigger proposals.

The more clarity you can bring about the business value of certain outcomes, the more you can charge for those outcomes.

How Do You Use Value-Based Project Pricing without Concrete Metrics?

Some clients won't share details about ROI, and thus you won't have concrete metrics to show. When you can't lean on that proof of past results, you must be that much more diligent in drawing out insights and details during the discovery conversations.

For example, a freelance writer might ask a prospect, "What are your top-performing posts? What did they do for your company? And if we were to put together posts that were just as good or better, what would that do for you?" Insights gleaned will help her quantify the approximate value of the desired outcome.

Remember, many clients don't quantify value with dollars and cents. Sometimes, they want to become a recognized authority: "We need content that positions our CEO as a leading authority and helps her land high-profile speaking gigs." Or, they want pride: "I finally have a website I'm eager to share." Or, they want relief and renewed passion: "Our brand's new visual identity reinforces the incredible work we do instead of detracting from it."

NINE COUNTERINTUITIVE MOVES
FOR LIFE-CHANGING FREELANCE INCOME

The value for the client can be as straightforward as less complexity and stress. If you've ever worked with a busy founder or C-suite leader, then you know they appreciate fewer demands placed on their time: "We need a designer who can meet us halfway with strategic thinking and visually communicate our intellectual property without tons of oversight."

Value depends on the client, so you quantify what matters most to them. Over the years, I've assembled a tool kit of consulting questions that help me isolate the value during the flow of conversation. Think of yourself as a prospector panning for gold. Each open-ended question swirls the sand and gravel until brilliant gold flecks appear:

- Why is this so important?
- What will be different once we finish this project?
- What do you think the current situation is costing you in terms of opportunities and revenue?

What if the discovery conversation leaves you with no bag of golden insights?

Default to your key differentiators. A freelance writer might anchor her value pricing in her industry expertise, versatility, effectiveness, and delightful process:

- Industry Expertise. "I've worked with a number of high-end med spas."
- Versatility. "I'm adept at learning each client's brand and bring your distinct voice, personality, and tone into everything I write."

- Effectiveness. "I'm a gifted good storyteller, interviewer, and researcher. I make pieces authoritative by citing industry experts, pulling in statistics, and weaving everything together into a compelling narrative."
- Process. "I'm a self-starter who can handle projects, beginning to end, with minimal oversight from you and very few demands on your time."

When all else fails, find a new market or target audience. One will place a higher value on your expertise and talent than another.

Marketing and copywriting legend Gary Halbert was fond of asking his students this question: "If you and I both owned a hamburger stand and we were in a contest to see who could sell the most hamburgers, what advantages would you most like to have on your side to help you win?"

He'd let the students give sensible answers before he dropped this bombshell: "The only advantage I want is A STARVING CROWD!"

In one of his Boron Letters, Halbert goes on to recommend one of the most profitable habits that freelancers can develop: "What I am trying to teach you here is to constantly be on the lookout for groups of people (markets) who have demonstrated that they are starving (or at least hungry!) for some particular product or service."[3]

In early 2023, I charged around $3,000 each for two case studies: twenty times what I charged when I first started freelancing. My talent hasn't grown exponentially, but I did identify a starving crowd: software consulting companies. The value of a single project can exceed $100,000. Anchored against that potential ROI, my fee for long-form, narrative case studies looked reasonable, not excessive.

Serve up your concrete metrics, value quantified through painstaking discovery, and key differentiators to a starving crowd, and you'll find it *much* easier to charge value-based prices.

What Is Your Approach to Time Tracking?

Tracking time is tedious. Do it anyway, even if you charge flat fees. Otherwise, how will you benchmark your effective hourly rate (EHR) for different tasks and projects?

Your biggest money isn't always your best money, and an accurate EHR will help figure out what type of projects pay you the best and which direction you want to put your marketing and growth.

If I'm Charging Hourly, How Do I Set Realistic Expectations with Clients about How Long Certain Tasks and Projects Should Take?

Many clients don't know how long tasks and projects take, and in the absence of information based on experience, they improvise, usually by pulling time estimates out of their derriere.

We can't stop clients from guessing, but we can propose as process that will supply the missing information.

I use language like this: Okay, so you're predicting fifteen hours. Here's the approach I recommend: I will write the first couple of emails, and I'll report back to you on how long they took me. If you are pleased with the quality of my work, then we'll use the first two emails to estimate the total time required and final price.

You must find a way to call out and counteract a client's wild guess. Otherwise, they'll take your silence as implicit agreement.

You must recalibrate expectations around hours, timeline, and budget early, so you don't leave the door open to frustration later.

A CMO and copywriter named Josh vented during our coaching call after of his more delusional clients had made a remark about a different copywriter who had turned around a campaign in a week.

Josh called him out:

Remember what happened when you hired that guy? His work wasn't very good, and the low quality put you behind, not ahead, of schedule. Are you after fast here or effective? You've already established that you can't have both.

The client saw Josh's point, but the exchange was one of the last straws. Josh later ended the relationship. Even if you can bring a client around to your point of view, the juice may not be worth the squeeze.

When a client throws out a wild guess, counter with a test. A test is both logical and reasonable. If that suggestion causes an adverse reaction in the other person, you know what type of person you're dealing with. Walk away.

NINE COUNTERINTUITIVE MOVES
FOR LIFE-CHANGING FREELANCE INCOME

What Is the Simplest Approach to Pricing You Can Recommend?

My friend Ed Gandia is a high-income business writing coach, and his idea of the Magic Quartile will serve you well when you don't have time for the more rigorous approach in this book:

> If you're really struggling, think of the absolute minimum you would want to charge, like the absolute floor—not a penny less would you be willing to accept. And then, think of the number that would be on the verge of creating panic for you. A penny more, and you would have a mental breakdown. But it's a number that you would be willing to quote. You wouldn't be able to do it confidently, but it's not outside the realm of possibility. Then, what you do is you take the average so you're right down the middle. And then, what I say is let's move into the Magic Quartile. The Magic Quartile would be a number that's just past that average, or the top third quartile. Right down the middle is a safe zone, but once you move a little bit past that into the top third Magic Quartile, you're really starting to push yourself and create a new normal. That's what I try to get people to do.[4]

Remember:

- There is no one-size-fits-all pricing "solution" for freelancers. Pricing models are neither good nor bad. They're simply tools that help you manage risk, maximize revenue, and strengthen your positioning.

- The hourly model minimizes risk in specific situations, but most of the time, it penalizes your skill, efficiency, and expertise.

- You'll only be satisfied with your freelance business long term if you charge based on the value you create.

- Most of your clients would rather fork over extra money than go through the hassle of replacing you.

- The right time to raise your prices is right now.

- If you raise your prices and lose a client, make the math work out in your favor. Spend your freed-up capacity on prospecting for the higher-paying clients you really want.

- The more clarity you can bring about the business value of certain outcomes, the more you can charge for those outcomes.

- Make your expertise obvious and unmistakable throughout your marketing, discovery, and sales process, and you won't need to justify your price later.

- Only once you and the client agree on the root problem, the project or path forward, and the desired outcomes do you start estimating your fees.

- Value depends on the client, so you quantify what matters most to them. Many clients don't quantify value with dollars and cents. Value can even be as simple as simplicity or less complexity and stress.

NINE COUNTERINTUITIVE MOVES
FOR LIFE-CHANGING FREELANCE INCOME

- The seven most common freelance pricing models are: Hourly, Flat Fee, Value-Based, Retainers / Subscriptions, Equity for Services, Fixed Timeframe, and Performance-Based.

- If you'd like to read a deeper analysis of all seven models, go to the Appendix. There, I break down the pros and cons and share tips for using each model effectively.

See you in Move Nine.

MOVE NINE:

Run Victory Laps

YOUR FINANCIAL NEEDS WILL EVOLVE WITH YOUR FREELANCE CAREER. Last year's exciting project fee will be this year's polite refusal. You'll revisit your prices many times. When you do, this condensed version of the pricing process will be waiting for you.

Time is money, after all.

Here's a checklist of key numbers:

- Survival Number
- True Availability
- Survival Rate
- Dream Number
- Dream Rate
- Pessimistic Price
- Weirdly Precise

Now, onto the process.

Find Your Survival Number

- Estimate your average monthly personal expenses.

    » The easiest way to do this is to export bank and credit card statements for the last three months—ideally, as a .csv file so you can use a formula to make quick work of the addition.

    » Add up ninety days' worth of transactions.

    » Divide the total by three to get an up-to-date monthly average for personal expenses.

- Add up your business-related spending.

    » Those of you who already have dedicated business checking and savings accounts can follow these steps:

    - Add up ninety days' worth of transactions.

    - Then, divide the total by three to get your up-to-date monthly average for business expenses.

    » Those of you who don't have dedicated business checking and savings accounts will need to revisit your personal statements:

    - Create a new Business Expenses tab in the spreadsheet.

    - Copy and paste all your expenses and delete all the personal ones.

- Use the list below to jog your memory and catch any sneaky ones you may have missed—e.g., apps you pay for with an annual subscription.

- Divide the total by three to get an up-to-date monthly average for business expenses.

You're going to forget something. The goal here is a ballpark number of what running the business costs each month.

Incomplete List of Business Expenses

- Administrative / office supplies (e.g., postage, printing, paper)
- Office space / overhead
- Internet service
- Phone / mobile service
- Tools (e.g., laptop)
- Software and subscriptions (e.g., email, web hosting, cloud storage, accounting software, time tracking, project management)
- Memberships (e.g., associations, industry groups)
- Local licenses and taxes
- Marketing
- Meals and entertainment (e.g., coffee with clients)
- Business travel / conferences

- Education and professional development (e.g., books, business coaching)
- Professional services (e.g., bookkeeping, tax prep, attorney fees, designer)

Figure Out Your Tax Percentage

To find your tax percentage, you have three options, with the first being the most reliable:

- Look at your last tax return. (Or ask your accountant to tell you.) For example, my CPA told me that my 2022 tax rate was 18.5 percent. Here are the three steps for freelancers paying US taxes:

    » Find your total income, usually on Line 9 of Form 1040. (For the one reader who cares, the total income number in your tax return will be close to the net income your accounting software shows for the year.)

    » Find your total tax, usually on Line 24 of Form 1040.

    » Multiply your total tax by 100, then divide that number by your total income.

- Ask two local freelancers with comparable income what their tax rate was, add their numbers, and divide by two to get your ballpark number.

- Make a conservative guess, such as 25 or 30 percent of your gross income.

Calculate Your Survival Number

- Subtract your tax percentage from 100. If your tax rate is 20 percent, then: 100 – 20 = 80. We'll call that 80 percent your After-Tax Revenue Percentage.

- Add up your personal and business expenses. This total represents the monthly "nut" you need to cover all bills. Let's say your personal expenses and business expenses add up to $3,000 a month.

- Multiply that number ($3,000) by 100: $3,000 × 100 = $300,000.

- Divide that number by your After-Tax Revenue Percentage (80 percent). $300,000 / 80 = $3,750. That's your monthly revenue target. You must earn $3,750 each month to cover your $3,000 monthly nut, set aside $750 for taxes, and essentially break even.

- Calculate your yearly Survival Number. $3,750 per month × 12 months = $45,000. You must make at least that much to avoid getting yourself into debt and financial trouble.

Here are my numbers: My family of five living in Knoxville, Tennessee, needs $9,000 each month, or $108,000 a year. That $108,000 is my Survival Number.

Find Your True Availability

- Figure out your available work weeks.

NINE COUNTERINTUITIVE MOVES
FOR LIFE-CHANGING FREELANCE INCOME

- » Add up the days in the next twelve months you will not work. Include holidays, vacation, sick days, and personal time off.
- » Divide the number of days by seven and round up.
- » Subtract that number from fifty-two to get available work weeks.
- » Here's what my scenario looks like: 52 weeks − 6 weeks off = 46 available work weeks

- Add up your available work hours in a week.
  - » Estimate the number of hours you work in a typical week. When do you usually start and stop working? How long do you take for lunch? Do you work on weekends? How much? Do you really want to work on Saturday and Sunday or do you tell yourself you have to? Is your current pace healthy, sustainable, and enjoyable?
  - » Do some quick math to figure out the hours you work in an average week—your "available" work hours.

- Calculate available time inventory.
  - » Multiply available work weeks by available work hours per week.

- Account for effectiveness.
  - » You've got to account for "effectiveness": the number of hours you can reasonably expect to spend on client

projects or hours you can bill to clients. This number will be smaller than your available work hours.

» Estimate the percentage of hours you can think you can effectively bill each week.

» Turn your percentage (e.g., 60 percent) into a decimal (e.g., 0.60).

» Multiply your available time inventory by the decimal. That number represents your annual billable hours.

Here are my numbers:

- 60 percent of my available hours spent on billable work is realistic for me.

- 1,748 work hours per year (my available time inventory) times 0.60 equals 1,048 billable hours.

- 1,048 hours represents my True Availability—that is, how many hours I'll have each year for billable work.

Find Your Survival Rate and Dream Number

- Find your Survival Rate.

    » Plug your numbers from previous exercises into this Survival Rate calculation: Annual Survival Number / Annual Billable Hours = Survival Rate

    » My Survival Rate calculation looks like this: $108,000 / 1,048 billable hours = $103.05 an hour. My Survival Rate is ≈$103.

NINE COUNTERINTUITIVE MOVES
FOR LIFE-CHANGING FREELANCE INCOME

- Find your Dream Number.
    - » Set a timer for fifteen minutes.
    - » Write down a meaningful amount of money per month for any of the categories below relevant to you:
        - Debt paydown (e.g., credit cards, student loans, car loan, mortgage)
        - Short-term saving (e.g., emergency fund, upcoming travel, holiday gifts)
        - Long-term saving (e.g., car, down payment, wedding)
        - Investing (e.g., retirement, real estate, stock, crypto)
        - Lifestyle goals (e.g., vacation home, RV, private school for kids)
        - Giving (e.g., faith community, nonprofits, causes, friends, family)
        - Bucket list (e.g., restoring a vintage Airstream, extended vacation in Japan)
        - Passion projects (e.g., recording an album, learning Spanish)
    - » Don't worry about creating a comprehensive list. All you're after right now is a ballpark number to help you do this calculation:

- Add up the numbers above. How much extra do you want each month to make progress on these financial and lifestyle goals?
- Multiply that number by twelve.
- Add that annualized total to your Survival Number. That's your Dream Number.

Example: Some of My Dreams:

For me to move past surviving to truly thriving would mean I was making definitive progress each month on these three specific, near-term goals:

- Emergency fund that covers at least six months' worth of my family's Survival Number
- Nice basement and pool for hosting and hanging out
- Writing cabin in the backyard

Find Your Dream Rate

To find your Dream Rate:

- Use the same math that produced your Survival Rate:

Annual Dream Number / Annual Billable Hours = Dream Rate

Example: My Freelance Dream Rate:

- 52 weeks a year – 6 weeks not working = 46 work weeks.

NINE COUNTERINTUITIVE MOVES FOR LIFE-CHANGING FREELANCE INCOME

- 46 work weeks per year × 38 average work hours per week = 1,748 work hours per year.

- 1,748 work hours × 0.60 (or, 60 percent effectiveness) leaves 1,048 billable hours.

- My Survival Number of $108,000 per year (or, $9,000 per month) / 1,048 billable hours = a Survival Rate of $103 per hour.

- A Dream Number averaged out to $3,750 extra per month, or $12,750 total per month, or $153,000 per year.

- My Dream Number ($153,000) / 1,048 billable hours gives me a Dream Rate of $146 per hour.

Set Your Pessimistic Price

- Pick a project and list the tasks.

  » Use these categories to jog your memory, and be sure to include time-suckers, such as calls, emails, and project management:

    ◆ Scheduling, project setup, and ongoing project management

    ◆ Communication, including emails, meetings, and phone calls

    ◆ Research and other prep work

    ◆ Actual creative work and deliverables

- Presentation, capturing feedback, making changes

- Admin work (e.g., project wrap-up, file delivery, and invoicing)

• Add up and round up the total time required.

» If you are new to freelancing or time tracking, write down your best guess for each task in fifteen-minute increments.

» If you have *tracked* your time during *previous projects*, this step will be straightforward for you:

- Log into your time-tracking app.

- Generate a report for a similar project.

- Cross-reference it with the task list you just created.

- Retroactively add time for any tasks or categories you didn't track.

» For example: writing a long-form, narrative case study for one of my clients might look like this:

- Send email with onboarding questionnaire:	0.25 hr.
- Do kickoff call:	1.0 hr.
- Schedule interviews:	0.25 hr.
- Set up project docs:	0.50 hr.

NINE COUNTERINTUITIVE MOVES
FOR LIFE-CHANGING FREELANCE INCOME

- Create outline and do initial research: 1.5 hrs.
- Conduct two 30-minute interviews: 1.00 hr.
- Have interviews transcribed: 0.25 hr.
- Write first draft: 4 hrs.
- Finalize first draft & send to client for review: 1.5 hrs.
- Work through client's feedback and revisions: 1 hr.
- Work through final edits and spell check: 0.75 hr.
- Send final draft to client: 0.25 hr.

Total: 12.25 hours

Rounded-up estimate: 13 hours

- Multiply total time by your Dream Rate.
  - » My first stab at a price for case study projects came to $1,898: 13 hours × $146 / hour = $1,898
- Add a buffer to get your Pessimistic Price.
  - » Build a 20 percent buffer into your price on the front end. Budget for human nature. Expect clients to be on their worst behavior, not their best.
  - » Multiply the initial price from the last step by 1.2.
- Gauge your enthusiasm.

» Once you have your Pessimistic Price, ask these questions:

- Would I be happy to make that amount of money for that amount of work?

- Is the price high enough to feel exciting, even a little risky?

- Does the price feel like a step forward for the business?

» If the price doesn't hold up under scrutiny, ask yourself:

- Why do I have misgivings?

- Does the price feel high or low?

- Is the price or my confidence the real problem?

- What would need to be true for me to feel good about this price?

» Adjust the price by small increments of $25 or $50 (or the equivalent in your local currency) until you've got a new price that feels better.

Make It Weirdly Precise

- Make the price weird.

    » Salt your prices with specificity. Change zeroes to $25 or $75. The extra, slightly higher amounts won't be enough to break the deal with the client and cost

NINE COUNTERINTUITIVE MOVES
FOR LIFE-CHANGING FREELANCE INCOME

you the project, but those same amounts can make a meaningful difference for your earning and financial stability, especially when you add them up across a year.

» Weirdly precise prices have consistently worked for me:

- $575 instead of $500 for 300 words of web copy
- $2,975 instead of $3,000 for a narrative, long-form case study
- $3,375 instead of $3,500 for a 1-Day Brand Sprint

Remember:

- Your pricing will change with your season of life, financial goals, and level of expertise and confidence.

- Don't fudge your numbers. Honor the pricing process. Be honest about what you really want to be making.

- Any amount you charge above your past prices is a win. We compete against our past rates, not our future ones.

CONCLUSION
◇◇◇◇◇◇◇◇◇◇◇◇

One of my family's traditions was a high school graduation gift of the child's choice. I chose a silver Gary Fisher mountain bike, and one Saturday soon after, with nothing better to do, I rode my bike across the street to a new subdivision.

The curves of the freshly paved asphalt road led up a hill to a faint trail disappearing into a small patch of woods. Intrigued, I followed it a short way until it ended abruptly at a once-beautiful Spanish-style villa, complete with a courtyard, fountain, and hand-painted tiles.

The villa looked like a place where a famous Hollywood director would throw fabulous parties. Fire had gutted it. Several exterior walls of the house itself looked as though a giant beast had taken huge bites out of them. They had blackened edges.

Feeling both fascinated and guilty, I explored that study in contrasts. Two carved wooden doors, ancient and obviously imported, stood untouched, yet when I turned in place, the rest of the room held sad, assorted wreckage. With the roof gone, rain had soaked everything. Beanie babies and vinyl records. Furniture and mail. All the stuff of family and life destroyed.

One envelope with an oval cutout caught my eye. My grandparents passed around similar ones at Christmas. I picked it up, and the face of Ben Franklin stared back at me. It took me a second to realize I was looking at a $100 bill, not Monopoly money.

I'd come across plenty of coins and dollar bills, maybe the odd twenty that blew out of an open car window, but never a hundred smackers.

Wow. Free money.

Then, another pang of guilt hit me. By taking the money was I profiting off someone else's misfortune?

A quick search in that room turned up no other address where I could send the money. That made sense. No family expects their house to burn down and leaves instructions. Maybe the family would have a forwarding address?

After running through options, I concluded that it was unlikely I could return the money and that no one would benefit if I left it where I had found it. On the other hand, many people would benefit if I took my friends bowling that night, treated them all to ice cream afterwards, and gave 10 percent to my church.

As I wrote this book, that experience kept coming back to me—not the tragedy of the fire, but the feeling of finding money and the realization that taking it hurt no one. That free-money feeling is a hard one to beat. It is buoyed by the thrill of possibilities suddenly unfolding, by the prospect of fun and generosity, spreading good fortune around so more people benefit.

The feeling has followed a soggy envelope, tax refund, and an unexpected prize. More recently, I have engineered it when selling big freelance projects, ones that I have charged less for in the past, ones that were too much fun to feel like work, ones where I was pleased with the outcome and the client was, too. Clients are happy to pay more when they believe the value is there, and their experience and the results never call that into question.

The best freelance projects feel like free money. Freelancing can be both joyful and profitable. If either the joy or profit is absent, or diminished, then we are clever, creative, and committed enough to suss out why and solve the problem.

My sincere hope is that this book will play a part in putting a dopey free-money smile on your face many times. The best is yet to come, friend.

Start Creating the Business and Lifestyle You Really Want

You now have the pricing methodology and know some of the principles and best practices for charging higher prices. Some freelancers will change their minds, change their prices, and change their lives. Why shouldn't you be one of them? Why not step up into a bigger vision for your work, creativity, and life?

Millions of value-conscious clients are happy to pay a premium for the right outcomes. Why shouldn't you be the freelancer or consultant to help them?

This transformation is easier with a seven-part framework I call the "$300K Flywheel." The framework is the distillation of fifteen years of trial and error and over $1.8 million earned as a creative entrepreneur while learning what not to do. Hundreds of freelancers and consultants have applied the concepts and have grown both their income and time freedom.

Instead of feeding more and more time into the business machine, you can join like-minded creative entrepreneurs who are stacking up the right advantages and finding their income-lifestyle sweet spot. Go to FreelanceCake.com/coaching to learn more about the Business Redesign program and apply.

APPENDIX

Resources

Books and Websites for Raising Your Financial Literacy

The Psychology of Money by Morgan Housel

I Will Teach You to Be Rich by Ramit Sethi

Rich Dad, Poor Dad by Robert Kiyosaki

The Millionaire Next Door by Thomas J. Stanley and William D. Danko

Your Money or Your Life by Vicki Robin and Joe Dominguez

Profit First by Mike Michalowicz

The Creative Professional's Guide to Money by Ilise Benun

You Are a Badass at Making Money by Jen Sincero

The Art of Money by Bari Tessler

MappedOutMoney.com with Hanna and Nick True

APPENDIX

Books and Websites for Rethinking Your Approach to Freelancing and Consulting

Million Dollar Consulting by Alan Weiss

The Business of Expertise by David C. Baker

The Win Without Pitching Manifesto by Blair Enns

The Go-Giver by Bob Burg and John David Mann

Give and Take by Adam Grant

Essentialism by Greg McKeown

FreelanceCake.com with Yours Truly

Seven Freelance Pricing Models, Plus Their Pros and Cons

Here are the seven most common freelance pricing models:

- Hourly
- Flat Fee (or, Fixed Price, Fixed Scope)
- Value-Based
- Retainers (or, Monthly Subscriptions)
- Equity for Services
- Fixed Timeframe (or, VIP Daily or Weekly Sprints)
- Performance-Based

APPENDIX

No One Size Fits All

Pricing models are neither good nor bad. Each one is simply a tool in your freelance kit. If you were in the kitchen and had both a watermelon and carrots to cut, you'd be wise to use a chef's knife for the former and a paring knife for the latter. You don't want to cut yourself. The right knife manages that risk.

There is no one-size-fits-all pricing "solution" for freelancers. That may be the most important takeaway in this book.

Every freelance and consulting gig comes with risks, some easy to predict and some hard. We must consider the client, project, and circumstances and pick the pricing model that accomplishes three things in that situation:

1. Manages risk.
2. Maximizes revenue.
3. Strengthens positioning.

Whoever Takes the Risk Gets the Upside

Keep in mind that your goal in freelancing isn't to mitigate risk entirely. Some risk can be good because whoever takes the risk gets the upside.

If you charge hourly, you pass the risk and the upside to the client. If the project takes longer than expected or the client keeps changing her mind, the price goes up. She took the risk, and she paid a higher price. On the other hand, if you do good work quickly, the client pays less for it. She took the risk, and she got the upside, which was a lower price.

If you charge a flat fee, you take the risk. For example, let's say a freelance writer ordinarily charges $100 an hour and expects to put ten hours into a white paper. The right opportunity comes along, and he decides to charge a flat fee of $1,000 instead. He takes the risk and gets the upside when the project takes eight hours. His efficiency pushes his effective hourly rate to $125, or 25 percent higher than usual.

Your risk tolerance will fluctuate. Sometimes, you'll feel audacious enough to throw out a higher number and let the chips fall where they may. Sometimes, more conservative prices will seem prudent to you: "I can't be super aggressive with my prices right now, broski. My kid needs braces!"

Engineer an Asymmetric Relationship

You don't need to beat yourself up. Playing it safe on occasion doesn't make you a second-rate freelancer. Also, be honest about what your conservatism can cost, long term. You'll only stay satisfied with your freelance business if you charge based on the value you create.

Keep searching for that value-focused pricing sweet spot. Engineer an asymmetric relationship between the time you put in and the money you get out.

APPENDIX

By all means, name an outrageous price on occasion. Clients will surprise you. Jonathan Stark, consultant and host of the Ditching Hourly podcast, reminds us that if our prices aren't offending someone, we're undercharging:

> Good pricing always seems outrageous to somebody. All that matters is that your prices are acceptable to your ideal buyers. It doesn't matter what your friends, family, colleagues, strangers on Reddit, or anyone else thinks. If nobody thinks your prices are outrageous, you haven't found your sweet spot yet.[1]

Okay, enough chitchat. Let's weigh the pros and cons of each model and look at a positive example of each one.

The Hourly Model

Charging hourly is the most common pricing model. In other industries it goes by the name of Time and Materials or Cost Plus. You get paid an hourly rate for your time, and you charge the client for any project expenses, such as website hosting or stock photo licenses.

Salty freelancers and consultants rail against the hourly model for good reason. With hourly you're trading time for money, and the main benefit of other models is that they're not hourly. They spring you from the trap.

Without a doubt, Hourly is the dull paring knife in your freelance kitchen, yet as I already mentioned, it can cut down on frustration with certain clients and projects. Let's examine the pros and cons.

APPENDIX

Here are the pros of the hourly model:

- Clients understand the hourly model. There's no explaining to do.

- It feels familiar and comfortable. Most people have had a past job that paid by the hour. In high school I made $7.50 an hour waiting tables in a retirement home. Serving fried catfish and tomato aspic to affluent octogenarians showed me what I didn't want to do with my life.

- Hourly is uncomplicated. The simplicity and transactional nature of hourly billing may appeal to you: Track every minute you put into meetings, emails, and the work, add your timesheets to invoices, and get paid for all the time you put in.

- This model provides an easy onramp for new freelancers. When you don't know how long certain projects may take or don't yet understand the intricacies of putting a price tag on creativity, expertise, and problem-solving, just charging hourly can be a relief.

- The hourly model works with flighty, disorganized, or indecisive clients. You may wonder how ten projects can all be the unfocused founder's "top priority," but each time he changes his mind, he feeds your invoices and makes them grow big and strong. Thanks, guy!

- It works with dumpster-fire clients. Some companies will subject you to broken processes. They'll make puzzling decisions, then reverse them, then reverse the

APPENDIX

reverse. Hourly ensures that the client pays for the chaos, dysfunction, and inefficiency, not you. When a project transmogrifies into a reverse-reversed Frankenstein, you send bigger invoices.

- Hourly works for projects that are hard to predict. Software development, websites, and project management come to mind. No matter how long you've been doing it, a near-infinite number of surprises and oopsies can change the scope. Two months into a new website build, the client may come to you, hat in hand, and say, "We forgot to tell you that our customers need to be able to book appointments." A twenty-one-hour wrestling match with the scheduling software's API ensues. Planning in advance for every such Herculean effort or every five-minute tweak would be tedious, if not impossible. Charging hourly enables you to navigate the inherent complexity and inevitable scope creep without putting your earning at risk.

The pros are enticing, yet for every situation where charging hourly has protected me, I can think of three where it hurt.

Here are the cons of the hourly model:

- Hourly caps your earning potential. Whether you charge $5 or $500 an hour, you're trading time for money. You can only raise your hourly rate so high before you start getting too many nos. You can only sell so many hours before you run out of "inventory." You can only leverage your productivity and work longer hours before you burn yourself out. The trouble with that burnout border is you usually only see it after you've crossed it.

- Hourly penalizes skill and efficiency. The faster you work, the less you earn. By contrast, the flat fee model rewards you for streamlined processes and delivering a positive outcome in less time. The faster you work, the more you earn.

- Hourly doesn't account for all the ways freelancers create value. Yes, we assemble words, move pixels, and write lines of code. We also learn through trial-and-error the nuances of copywriting, identity design, and software engineering. As best practices shift, true expertise adapts. What price tag can a client put on good taste or incisive judgment? On sensitive leadership or out-of-the-box strategy? On the one brilliant idea that became the linchpin of the whole marketing campaign? Some freelancers and consultants can solve a problem in ten minutes that would take one of their peers ten hours. With hourly you don't profit from your X factor.

- Hourly turns you into a commodity. Time is never what a freelance client buys. They want outcomes. They want their problems to disappear. Naturally, that doesn't stop them from comparing the freelance email copywriter who charges $50 an hour to the one who charges $150 an hour. Even if you deliver three times or ten times as much value, you still face an uphill negotiation. Ultimately, it's better to quantify the value of the client's

APPENDIX

desired outcome, anchor a fixed fee against that value, and opt out of the hourly game altogether.

Use these questions to decide if you should charge hourly for your next project:

- Is this project with a past client who wants to reengage? If so, has the client asked for lots of changes and revisions in the past? Has scope creep been a problem? Hourly might not be a bad idea.

- Does this person or company have inefficient or broken processes? Lots of extra time, difficulty, or irritation may make hourly the safer bet. Or you may need to choose sanity over money and pass on the project altogether.

- Does the prospect seem disorganized, scattered, or indecisive? Do they struggle to set priorities or clearly articulate needs? Maya Angelou once said to Oprah Winfrey, "When people show you who they are, believe them the first time."[2] Those process and personality challenges you notice? Chances are, they will persist, and it's not your responsibility to facilitate marathon discovery sessions for free. Sell a paid discovery session or a time block of ten or twenty hours. Pass the risk to them or pass on the project.

- After one or more discovery conversations, do you seem to be no closer to defining what the project is? See above. Charge for formal, paid discovery.

APPENDIX

- Does the prospect struggle to answer practical questions about the scope or go off on tangents? This is called wasting your time. See above.

- Is the prospect hard to pin down or slow to respond to emails? This will continue. See above.

- Does the client have significant or problematic gaps in knowledge? If the client doesn't understand realistic timelines, best practices, good workflow, or the nature of the work you do, remember that extra education and handholding chews through time and good humor. See above.

- Has the client said or done anything that suggests lots of "personality management" will be necessary? Some prospects will seem incapable of giving you concrete plans or clear instructions: "I'm the visionary type. I have a lot of amazing ideas. I just need someone to implement them." In those situations, my snarky teenager side can't help but think, "Yeah, sure, you're the next Elon Musk, but I still don't know you want me to do." Unless you enjoy the confusion and frustration of moving targets, see above.

You may decide hourly is the right tool for the project, client, or situation because you can't stomach the risk or really need the work. Fine. Be practical.

Just don't forget that other pricing models have more financial upside and offer more long-term satisfaction.

APPENDIX

Four Tips for De-Risking the Hourly Model

- Use a minimum engagement. Some clients will ask for a small project or handful of easy tasks. You can use "minimum engagements" to avoid sending piddly, half-hour invoices. I have approached these engagements in two ways: (1) use the lowest project price I'm willing to accept, or (2) sell a time block of ten or twenty hours. With the latter, you track your time and knock out whatever the client needs. Any time they don't use rolls forward as a credit toward future projects.

- Track your time. Every minute you spend on a client project is one you should track. I know, I know, remembering to start the timer and add notes becomes tedious, yet diligence pays now (getting paid for all the time you spend) and later (using a past project to accurately predict the time required for a similar one and quoting a flat fee).

- Invoice every two weeks. You don't want to spring a hefty bill on clients at the very end of the project. Even if you were just doing what they asked, the higher-than-expected price can end an otherwise successful project on a sour note. By invoicing twice a month, you get paid more often. This helps with cash flow and helps both parties keep tabs on a project's cost. Fewer surprises means happier clients.

- Charge a rush rate. When a client comes to you with a tight deadline, do you tie on your superhero cape and start right away? Or do you say, "Sorry, I have prior

APPENDIX

commitments and can't make this my top priority"? Assuming the tight deadline still affords enough time to do work you're proud of, you have a third option: Charge a rush rate or expedite fee for faster delivery. Airlines do it by charging extra for priority boarding. FedEx does it with overnight packages. Disney does it at their theme parks. You can pay extra to skip the lines. A rush rate enables you to serve clients in a tight situation without sending the wrong message: "Come to me with your emergencies. I'll drop everything and walk you to the front of the line."

Positive Example of the Hourly Model: Complicated Company

One longstanding client of mine was a multi-national medical device manufacturer. I worked with a marketing director who oversaw several small business units. We agreed that I would be charge by the hour and round up to the nearest fifteen-minute increment. She agreed to let me bill for large blocks of hours in advance.

Boy, was I glad I did! Simple copywriting and design projects took on a comical inefficiency and complexity, thanks to time zone differences, language and cultural barriers, vague pecking orders, and baffling decision-making protocols.

One discount and rebate guide for sales reps went through over fifteen iterations.

Another time, I rushed to edit email content sent to me last minute only to be told afterward that they would be using the

APPENDIX

original typo-ridden version. Why? It had already been approved by the same higher up who wrote it. Three cheers for bureaucracy and botched email newsletters!

I remember thinking, "How is this company still in business?"

Thanks to charging hourly, I was able to keep most of the madness at arm's length. Every round of edits put more money in my pocket.

The Flat Fee Model (or Fixed Price, Fixed Scope)

Once you're confident that you can give accurate fixed-price quotes, do that instead.

Charging a flat fee helps you to engineer an asymmetric relationship between time and money. When you end up finishing the project in six hours instead of twelve, your effective hourly rate (EHR) doubles. The faster you work, the more you make. You reward your skill, efficiency, and expertise.

Let's start with the pros:

- This model reassures clients. Some clients don't like the hourly model because of the uncertainty it represents: No matter what the estimate says, how much is the project *really* going to cost? A flat fee is less ambiguous and risky. The price is the price.

- Flat Fee rewards expertise. Clients don't care how the sausage is made. Whether a $5,000 project takes you

APPENDIX

three hours or twenty is inconsequential. They get what they paid for. As you button up your processes and deliver better outcomes in less time, your EHR goes up.

- Flat Fee weakens the relationship between time and money. You'll often hear freelance pros declare, with *feeling*, "Stop trading time for money!" Well, there's no such thing as fully passive income. You'll *always* trade time for money, but you can make strategic decisions to lower your time input and raise the income output. Optimizing for that asymmetric relationship will make your business more enjoyable and sustainable. If twenty hours of billable work per week can cover your immediate needs and long-term financial goals, you can do whatever you want with the rest of your time. Did someone say four-day weekends?

- Flat Fee compensates us for the full spectrum of ways we create value. We work with our hands and our heads, and we deserve to be compensated for the many ways we make our clients' lives and business better—for example, our domain expertise, judgment, taste, and leadership.

- Flat Fee strengthens your positioning. Clients know freelancers aren't identical widgets, but the Hourly model encourages easy (and often unfair) comparisons based on price. A flat fee shifts the focus from price to value. What will the client get and what is that worth? That expanded focus creates opportunities to show your expertise, quality, and process—who you are and how

APPENDIX

you do what you do. The client gets so much more than your time and hard skills.

With the upside comes risk. Here are Flat Fee's cons:

- Inaccurate time estimates can burn you. If you haven't sold a similar project in the past or if you didn't track your time closely, your best guess is just that, a guess. Once the project starts, you may discover, to your chagrin, that your guess was a little off (or on a different continent). Ten hours become twenty, yet you must still finish the project. That miscalculation cut your EHR in half. It stings, believe me.

- Projects evolve. That's just what they do. Another stakeholder enters the fray. New information comes to light. Goal posts move. Those of you who have charged flat fees know the twang of mental tension you feel as you try to minimize the time you put in (to protect your EHR) while also navigating changes and surprises and delivering a positive outcome. When should you let the buffer you built into your price absorb minor scope creep? And when should you draw the line and have a frank conversation with the client? When scope creep shows its beady-eyed face, you can't be squeamish. Broaching the subject of scope creep can be uncomfortable, but maintaining healthy boundaries and not doing extra work for free is one of the practices that separates the amateurs from the professionals.

APPENDIX

Positive Example of the Flat Fee Model: Copywriting for a Video Script

After my filmmaker friend landed a new project, he looped me in to write a three- to five-minute Kickstarter video script. Because I'd written scripts, I knew about how long I'd need to finish the project.

I didn't know much about the client's personality or personality, so I added plenty of cushion to my quote, which was $2,000.

The client said yes, the project went smoothly, and all told, I spent just shy of three hours on drafts, edits, and meetings.

The client never would have agreed to pay me $667 an hour, yet that's what I made.

Lesson learned: Sell outcomes, not hours.

The Value-Based Model

The best clients won't care how much time you put into the project. They won't care if your EHR is $40, $400, or $4,000. What matters is the felt, smile-sparking absence of their problems or the value of whatever outcome you helped them achieve.

A local nonprofit may capture $100,000 more in donations after you help them rethink their strategy and update their website's UI/UX, along with the stories, photos, videos, and copywriting. A similar strategy project for an e-commerce company may generate ten times more value, an extra $1,000,000 in sales.

Based on the industry or context, the value of the project's outcome goes up or down. Your value-based price should, too.

Some freelancers (and more consultants) develop a sixth sense for this sliding scale and anchor the project's price against potential ROI. You should, too.

Let's start with the pros of the Value-Based model:

- Value-Based pays you for your X factor, not your time. A copywriter goes on a five-minute walk and comes back with a genius turn of phrase. In thirty minutes, a senior software engineer uncovers and fixes a bug that two of her peers couldn't root out in eight hours. You can and should be paid handsomely for solving painful, expensive problems, and if you're able to do that in a fraction of the time, all the better for you.

- Value-Based pays for your many aptitudes, not just your skills. Back in 2016, offering project and content road-mapping as a standalone engagement transformed my freelance business. The pivot to more "head work" led me to where I am today: a fractional Chief Marketing Officer (CMO) who sells advice in the form of leadership, strategy, planning, prioritization, and decision-making. Advisory services may seem like a far cry from the blog posts I used to write, but the aptitudes were always there. They needed time to grow, varied experience to deepen, and domain expertise and confidence to shore them up. Many freelancers aren't accustomed to getting paid for their ideas and advice, but more and more are figuring out what consultants have known all along: much of our hands work requires significant head work, and you can get paid a lot more when you swim up the value stream and use your many aptitudes, not just your creative skills, to help founders and executive leaders sharpen their thinking and solve painful, expensive problems. Domain expertise, research, curiosity, analysis, synthesis, new insights, resourcefulness, and good judgment have significant value. You can make bank with lucid thinking.

- Value-Based can dramatically reduce the hours you work. Once you get the hang of value-based pricing and sell a few projects, you don't need to hustle nearly as hard to hit your income target. You'll still need to market your offers, but as long as you deliver the desired outcomes and keep clients happy, you can spend less time overall on client work and put more of that blessed white space in your calendar.

Here are the cons:

- The value of certain projects is difficult to quantify. If you're a sales trainer, you can, with little effort, estimate the ROI of working with you. How many leads does the company get each month? What's the close rate and average deal value? Incremental improvements might produce $5 million in "recaptured" revenue for a new B2B client. For you to charge 10 percent,

APPENDIX

or $500,000, over a twelve-month period, would be reasonable. Freelance creatives, such as writers, designers, photographers, may have a harder time quantifying the value of ghostwriting op-ed articles for executives or creating a new identity system for a new direct-to-consumer salsa brand. It can be done, but it's hard. The knowing comes through doing. As you learn the ropes of quantifying value for each client and anchoring your price against that value, you may fumble a proposal or two. You may lose a project. Growth always comes with a cost.

- Big price tags shed light on head trash. You may have heard the axiom, "New levels, new devils." When we worry about overreaching and failing, we feed our imposter syndrome, overthinking, second guessing, perfectionism, procrastination. The more you charge, the higher the stakes. (At least that's the way it feels in the beginning.) Value-based pricing will bring to light your limiting beliefs and punctuate the need to upgrade your mindset. I know this because I still have to take my head trash to the curb daily!

- Some clients don't get value-based pricing. If they've worked with freelancers who charge hourly or a flat fee that was close enough for comfort, then your quote may confuse or upset them. I mentioned before that a prospect once called my prices "inflated" in an email: "The main hold up will be the price tag. Just to be transparent, it seems inflated, when the artwork and heavy lifting will come from us." I responded with a question: "What are you comparing my price to? Based on my past experience and research, my price for strategy, story development, and copywriting falls somewhere in the middle of the spectrum." I then shared five prices from competitors' websites to back up what I had just said. Did he come around? No, and that was okay with me. Half of winning at the value-based game is keeping your cool, figuring out how to stand your ground, and being prepared to walk away. The best negotiators don't need the deal.

Value-Based Pricing? This Means War.

Discussions about value-based pricing stir up strong feelings, er, opinions. When freelancers duke it out over "realistic" prices or "fairness" to clients, they're pointing to two distinct paradigms.

One such discussion unfolded in the comments after I published what I thought was a funny, relatable LinkedIn post: "That moment after a freelance client gives you an instant yes and you know you left money on the table."

One freelance writer implied that charging more when the opportunity arises was sneaky or dishonest—in his words, "getting away with it." He continued: "[Clients will] realize you're overcharging and move to someone with more realistic rates."

A second freelance writer questioned his logic: "So if you knew Client A would likely go on to make $100K from your time together and Client B [would make only] $5K, you would still charge them the same?"

APPENDIX

The first writer understood Paradigm One: the price depends on time and market dynamics.

- You charge based on the amount of time you put in.
- What other freelancers / consultants charge (market dynamics) also affects what you can charge.
- Client A may have higher upside with your work than Client B. That doesn't mean you provided more value.
- You shouldn't charge more just because you can. Even if you can get away with it, clients may feel like you overcharged and leave.

The second writer understood Paradigm Two: the price depends on perceived value and potential ROI.

- How much time you put into a project is irrelevant.
- Freelance / consulting projects don't have set prices. What people will pay changes with perceived value.
- Perceived value goes up with perceived expertise.
- Client A may make $100K from one case study you wrote, and Client B, only $5k. Because Client A has higher upside, you have delivered more value. It's fine to have a sliding scale based on the value you create.
- Client A may assign much lower value to your work if you charge less.

Both writers championed their paradigm. Both believe theirs was the right and reasonable one. Though I'm not here to bash the

APPENDIX

first writer, I will be blunt and say that you won't succeed with the Value-Based model until you believe that charging based on the value you create is right, good, and fair.

Why will some people pay $1,000 for a meal at a Michelin-starred restaurant and others would scoff at $100? Why will some people pay $25,000 for a watch and other people shrug and say, "My phone tells me the time"?

Different people put different values on different things. Duh.

The Value-Based model exists because it works. To some prospects, it's obvious, logical, and attractive.

Once you see that your low, "realistic" rates send the wrong signal to these value-conscious clients who are seldom motivated to save money, just because, you can't unsee it.

Other prospects won't know what value-based pricing is. They won't be receptive. Your "reasonable" price will make their eyes pop out of their heads. They may take your "ridiculous" price as a punch in the gut. Though you can explain your rationale, don't expect to change their minds.

Their disappointment that you're suddenly out of reach may morph into anger or disgust. Don't let that emotional reaction discourage or deter you.

Value-based pricing is a sifting tool which reveals which clients don't have the right value- and outcome-focused mindset, and which ones do.

Clients who are a good fit for value-based pricing meet these criteria:

APPENDIX

- They can focus more on value than price. If I offered to give you $10,000 for $2,000, you'd be stupid to say no. Yet, some clients will still try to find someone who will do "it" for $500 or $1,000. (Of course, "it" is never constant.) Some clients always choose the cheapest option. It's like a business tic. They can't help but ask for a discount. They'll drive thirty minutes across town to save $0.10 per gallon of gas. You're looking for outcome-focused clients who see the difference between expenses and investments and focus more on ROI.

- They have a well-defined business model. They could fill in Strategyzer's Business Model Canvas with relative ease.[3] They tend to know their customer segments, core offerings, value propositions, revenue streams, marketing channels, and cost structure. They see relationships between inputs and outputs. More effort invested in a leveraged opportunity, such as better email marketing, will likely produce a good result. People who understand their business model and its many relationships also see the upside in hiring a specialist to pull a specific lever.

- They have painful, expensive problems. Some problems aren't painful enough to solve. For example, an engineering firm may have a shockingly bad website. They won't spring for a gorgeous new website because the pain of the problem isn't acute enough because one of the managing partners is freakishly good at sales. Also, certain markets and companies of a certain size will place lower value on certain outcomes. A two-person micro-agency selling $5,000 websites won't place high enough

APPENDIX

value on a case study to pay $2,975. A consulting firm selling $100,000 engagements might. If one case study nets them one sale, their ROI would be 3,000 percent. The problem, market, or company must have a painful and expensive enough problem to precipitate desire for change. Doing nothing must be more expensive than hiring you.

- They have acute awareness of their problems or opportunities. I just mentioned shockingly bad websites. Some companies do need a beautiful, modern, responsive site. Even if you generate a report and show them their bounce rate, they'll ignore the opportunity cost. I once did a one-off consultation with a medical practice whose website was last month's garbage with last decade's computer monitors on top. It wasn't HIPAA compliant, and one would think that the fine for "willful neglect" would motivate them to put the money down for a new site. One would be wrong. Thankfully, some of your prospects will see the threats and opportunities, feel the urgency, and align their spending with long-term thinking.

- They pay attention to their numbers. You'll find it much easier to sell an e-commerce optimization consulting to a founder who already keeps tabs on key metrics, such as traffic sources, conversions, and average order value. If you can help your clients quantify the value of raising or lowering certain numbers, then the math can do the selling for you. Selling value-based engagements to

APPENDIX

people who don't know and track their KPIs, OKRs, and TL;DRs is much harder.

- They're tired of shoddy work. I'm not trying to knock anyone, especially beginners. We all have to start somewhere. But some projects do succeed or fail based on a freelancer's incisive thinking, attention to detail, deep expertise, and character. Sales copy, brand development, and software products come to mind. If you've ever tried to build a brand or app with amateurs, you know just how costly amateurs can be. For every dollar you saved, you spend two fixing their mistakes and messes. In the startup world lost time can be even more devastating than lost cash. Some clients get burned, say enough is enough, and fork over hefty fees for a veteran. It's hard to put a price on true expertise and the relief and peace of mind it represents to beleaguered clients.

Positive Example of the Value-Based Model: Business Plans for CEOs

One of my early coaching clients was a business consultant named Robert Cross. Robert's consulting clients hired him to help them fix expensive problems. The trouble was, he'd prove himself so capable that they kept delegating more and more to him. The predictable cashflow was nice, but too much low-level implementation work was starting to wear on him.

Consulting with C-level leaders was how Robert made his highest and best contribution. He knew that many CEOs of startups and small businesses were too busy and reactive. They lacked a clear, scalable business model.

Robert and I developed new positioning, messaging, and structure for two offers for those CEOs. Here was Robert's bold promise: "I help CEOs escape tactical hell and gain real traction in ninety days."

Robert had been charging $125 an hour. He wanted to pivot to value-based pricing. We used a more aggressive "internal" rate of $500 an hour to calculate a fixed price for both offers.

Within five weeks, Robert had sold his $10,000 offer to six new clients.

The Subscriptions Model (or Monthly Retainer)

Over the years I've sold a variety of subscriptions, which also go by the name of "retainer." "Retainer" is a carryover from the legal world where a company pays an attorney to be available in case the company needs counsel or suddenly finds itself in hot legal water.

Many of my clients weren't familiar with the term, so I started using a more common one: subscriptions. Everyone has one and knows what they are.

For freelancers and consultants, a subscription is a recurring monthly engagement consisting of a set of deliverables at a fixed cost, set of responsibilities, or certain availability.

APPENDIX

Technically, a subscription isn't an entirely different pricing model. It's simply a frequency (monthly) combined with one of the other models (typically, Hourly, Flat Fee, or Value-Based).

As for what can go into a subscription, you're limited only by your creativity. Time blocks, strategy sessions, specific deliverables, unlimited design projects and revisions, being "on call" and ready to delivery any variety of advisory services—it's all up for grabs. I've sold content marketing retainers, strategy subscriptions, and fractional CMO engagements that enable me to draw from my broad background in agencies, startups, and leadership roles across industries.

Here are the pros of the Subscriptions model:

- Subscriptions help you regulate cash flow. The main benefit of is making your cash flow more predictable without having to renegotiate the contract each cycle. Predictable monthly infusions of cash help you stabilize your business finances. Once you stack up enough subscriptions, you no longer feel the feast-or-famine extremes that freelancers bemoan. There's a reason many freelancers treat retainers and subscriptions as the holy grail. When you combine them with value-based pricing, you'll find yourself singing the Katrina and the Waves song, "Walking on Sunshine."

- Subscriptions hit the pressure release valve on sales. Make no mistake, you'll always be marketing and selling. However, stack up enough of subscriptions, and you can hit your monthly revenue target and lessen the urgency, month after month, to land and complete one-off projects. You'll experience less whiplash from mode shifts between sales and fulfillment, too. Eventually, you can be more selective and turn away one-off projects that you're not excited about.

- Subscriptions start you down the productized path. Subscriptions give you a clear incentive to carve off part of an open-ended service and deliver it monthly, and then develop well-defined standard operating procedures (SOPs) to deliver the same or better results in less time. This opens the door to effective delegation—did someone say virtual assistant and subcontractors?—and you spending more time in the flow of the work you most enjoy.

Here are the cons of Subscriptions model:

- Subscriptions can vanish. No matter how airtight, rock-solid, or bulletproof your service agreement is, some clients will still ignore the terms. They'll cancel their subscription unexpectedly, without cause. Your agreement may "protect" you in that situation. It may stipulate that the client must pay part or all the outstanding subscription fees. Yet, if the client goes dark or simply refuses to pay their balance, are you going to drag them to court? Probably not. You must decide whether the juice is worth the squeeze, and you'll most likely decide to cut your losses. If several clients pause or cancel subscriptions in quick succession, you may see income you were counting on vanish (and a sales pipeline that has barely a trickle moving through it).

APPENDIX

- Subscriptions can make us complacent. Many freelancers are so accustomed to winning the next project that we don't provide the best level of service to our most loyal clients. (Never *you*, of course. I'm talking about *other* freelancers.) The trick is not falling asleep on the job. Be as enthusiastic and industrious about keeping their business as you were about winning it. Rigorous process helps you deliver excellent outcomes and client experience month after month.

- The scope of subscriptions can get fuzzy, fast. During slower months, a client may not extract the full value from a subscription. What happens then? Does the unused allotment of your time or capacity disappear or does it roll forward as a "credit"? A slow accumulation of these credits can put you in a pickle later if a client decides to "redeem" them all during a month when you're spread thin. Ambiguity is the enemy here. You must explicitly state exactly how you handle these situations. In my experience, a "use it or lose it" policy is best for you, though some clients won't like it.

- Subscriptions can be boring. The knife cuts both ways. The very work that is well-defined and predictable can quickly lose its shine. The money's great, but where are the fresh creative challenges? When it comes time to ramp up for yet another month of X, Y, and Z, you find your gumption is noticeably non-gumptious. (As mentioned, the solution isn't to blow up all your subscriptions but to create better SOPs, hire subcontractors or staff, and delegate.)

APPENDIX

Positive Example of the Subscriptions Model: Strategy as a Service

Back in 2018, I started selling deep brand development engagements. Once we finished the work on the brand foundation and strategy, most clients were still new to brand management. New questions and needs would crop up:

- How did brand values affect who they hire?
- How did brand purpose influence what new products or services they should create?
- How should they think about brand architecture before launching those new products or services?

I had the idea of bundling a strategy subscription with the initial branding work. Together, the client and I would define what the brand is, and then I become the de facto brand manager and give the clients the ongoing support they needed through two strategy sessions per month.

That subscription—$1,750 per month for six months—doubled the value of most engagements and positioned me to get more repeat business and better case studies, too.

The Equity for Services Model

On occasion a client may ask you to "work on the come," meaning work now and get paid later. This ask is especially common from startup founders who need top-tier creative and consulting talent they can't always afford.

APPENDIX

"We're on a startup budget" is a nice way of saying "We can't afford your expertise and quality. We don't want to insult you by underpaying you. Would you consider helping us out anyway now in exchange for some upside later?"

To entice you to lend a head and hand, a prospect may offer a percentage of equity (that is, an ownership stake) in exchange for free work or discounted rates.

Out of all the pricing models we've covered, Equity for Services has the most risk and the most upside. (Remember, whoever takes the risk gets the upside.)

This model is usually a bad idea for a simple reason: Most startups fail.

Look up the statistics. The likelihood that your investment of talent and time will eventually become worth far more than whatever you would have charged in regular ol' fees is very low. Less than 10 percent.

Treat any Equity for Services deals as exactly what they are, a gamble, and don't make any bet you can't afford to lose.

Getting paid nothing up front isn't tenable for most of us, and that's why I recommend asking for a combination of cash fees, profit share, and equity, if you can swing it. For example, let's say the EHR you're going for is $150. The startup can realistically pay half that. You use $75 an hour to calculate your project fees, but they agree to pay you the second half over time, through quarterly profit shares. Maybe, they agree to pay an additional premium, too. Instead of $150, you make $250 an hour.

APPENDIX

When the honeymoon phase is over, you will want a relationship that made short- and long-term sense. (And hopefully, you'll still like the people you're in bed with.)

Under no circumstances should you do free work in exchange for compliments and promises. People don't respect things they get for free, and like other human beings, founders forget the details of what they committed to. Get everything in writing.

Stern warnings aside, here are the pros of the Equity for Services model:

- Equity can be worth more than cash. If you pick the right startup and do the right deal with them, equity later can be worth ten times, a hundred times, more than your cash fees.

- Equity and cash fees can go together. There's no reason you can't get some cash in the short-term and ask for profit shares and / or equity, too. You might as well ask for all three and see what happens.

- Opportunities create opportunities. Once you get in with the right set of startup founders and develop a reputation for doing high-quality work and being open to equity, word will get out. Opportunities beget opportunities.

Here are the cons:

- Most startups fail. The business will probably flounder before your equity is worth anything. I don't mean to be the bearer of bad tidings but look it up. Go in with your

APPENDIX

eyes wide open and recognize that equity for services is a bet with much worse odds than a coin toss.

- You count on the founders to eventually get you paid. Owning a small slice of a startup sounds cool, yet it's difficult to build a profitable business. It's even more difficult to build a business with enough value and momentum to attract outside interest. Your equity won't be worth anything (except a tax liability) until you either receive profit distributions (which you must negotiate as a part of your agreement) or until an investor or another entrepreneur buys part or all of the company and triggers a liquidity event. So, my friend, how much do you trust these founders? How would you rate their leadership and capabilities? Do you understand how the business will generate revenue and profit? Do you see and believe in the bigger opportunity? What's going on in the broader competitive landscape? I did the startup thing from 2013 to 2017 and discovered firsthand just how hard this is. Our startup reached the end of its lifecycle (meaning, it failed), and over four years, the startup paid me less than $3,000. And I was the co-founder!

- Equity isn't free. Equity, in essence, makes you an owner. You may not have voting or governance rights, and any number of people with different rights or a different class of shares may stand in front of you in line when a "liquidity event" happens. But as soon as you accept equity and the ink dries, you have business partners, with all the headaches pertaining thereto. Beyond the relational and emotional dynamics, you must think about the tax liability. Based on what happens with the company's valuation and spending over time, you may be looking at taxes even if you don't sell your shares or realize any gains. Before you sign anything, have a frank conversation with your accountant. Better yet, have more than conversation.

Positive Example of the Equity for Services Model

My friend Darrell Vesterfelt wanted to be an angel investor, but he didn't have the cash to invest. He did have his time, and he had spent years developing his skills and network.

All three had value to a to ConvertKit, a SaaS company. In exchange for equity, Darrell agreed to take a lower salary in ConvertKit's Head of Growth role.

Several years later, ConvertKit's founder Nathan Barry decided to sell a small percentage of the company at a valuation of $200 million. Darrell jumped at the opportunity to liquidate his shares. He has since used the proceeds to invest in other companies.

I'm happy for Darrell, and remember, his story is highly unusual.

The Fixed Timeframe Model

This model is a variation of Flat Fee and Value-Based. A client buys a half-day, day, week, or month instead of a project with a well-defined scope.

APPENDIX

Fixed Timeframe has been a common model in consulting and software development for years. Both types of work often require full immersion in the problem. They monopolize the consultant's engineer's attention, so daily or weekly billing makes sense. That's especially for consultants who may travel to work on-site with their client and charge a per-diem rate for travel days.

Of late, more freelance creatives are waking up to the possibilities. Several savvy practitioners, including Sarah Masci and Jordan Gill, have helped to popularize day rates, or "VIP days," with designers and web developers.

I've used Fixed Timeframe to sell a variety of workshops and 1-Day Brand Sprints.

Here are the pros of the Fixed Timeframe model:

- Fixed Timeframe simplifies marketing and sales. It's easy to break down your monthly revenue target into the exact number of projects, or days, you need to sell, and reverse-engineer your sales and marketing activities from there.

- Fixed Timeframe simplifies workflow. Scheduling is straightforward. You reserve certain days and spots in your calendar for a three-hour workshop here and a VIP Day there, and scope creep rarely becomes an issue.

- Outcomes are predictable. True, this model requires you to have a deep understanding of your area of focus, such as copywriting, branding, or design. You must also have the confidence to define steps, tasks, and even pre-work for clients and to complete several small projects or exercises quickly the day of. However, once you create a solid onboarding process, Fixed Timeframe represents less uncertainty, ambiguity, and risk than a regular project. Because six to eight hours isn't much time, you're less likely to overpromise and more likely to overdeliver.

- You can charge a premium. A client who would never pay you $300 an hour just might pay you $2,000 for a well-positioned VIP Day. The right offer for the right audience can raise your effective hourly rate dramatically.

Here are the cons of the Fixed Timeframe model:

- You need strong positioning, trust, and strong marketing and sales assets—ideally all three. To charge a premium for Fixed Timeframe, clients need to feel understood and see proof you can deliver. Or they need to lean on the trust you've earned during past projects. Or they need to see visuals, read what you've written about the process, and receive enough education to override their reservations and spark excitement. If you don't have the positioning, trust, and sales tools, then Fixed Timeframe will be an uphill scramble until you do.

- You must lead and occasionally say no. Clients want to get their money's worth, and some will try to pack in more tasks, projects, and desired outcome. Every new item you agree to raises expectations for the day as a whole and leaves you with less margin to knock out the two or three most important priorities. At times, you must step up and say no to create more space for key objectives and protect a positive outcome. Saying no and risking the client's temporary displeasure may make

APPENDIX

you squirm, but this type of foresight and leadership is a must.

- You will underestimate the time required. Any number of factors can double or triple the time needed to complete a task. Installing and configuring that website plug-in may take two hours when you only allotted one. Slicing photos for a new web page may send you on a wild goose chase for the original high-res version. You've already experienced Parkinson's law: Work expands to fill the time available. If you reach the end of the fixed timeframe without having met all your commitments: You know what to do. Finish what you started. Happy clients come back for more.

Positive Example: Consulting with Digital Agencies

Various consultants use a day rate as a minimum engagement for clients who need a little help in a lot of areas. In an interview with Chris Do, David C. Baker shared his experience charging Chris's friend $10,000 for a single day and three follow-up phone calls.[4]

The friend, Fabian Geyrhalter, described his engagement with David as transformative. It became a turning point in his career as a brand strategist and entrepreneur, and the value he received from the experience validated a remark Chris made: "Expensive is relative."

Chris went on to provide helpful reframing for the right value-based, fixed timeframe offer: Find the clients who can't

APPENDIX

afford to not work with you and sell them an outcome they really want in a fixed or accelerated timeframe.

Note: By 2020, David C. Baker had increased his day rate to $18,000, and in 2023, the price of his firm Punctuation's Total Business Reset flagship offering starts at $25,000. For some creative and digital firms, that price will be a bargain. Expensive is relative.

The Performance-Based Model

With this model, you get paid more when the project you're working on generates more revenue. It works in specific situations where the freelancer or consultant is so confident in their abilities that they'll charge a percentage of revenue or profit rather than up-front fees.

Those situations include the setup and management of ad campaigns, product launches (say, on a crowdfunding platform like Kickstarter), conversion copywriting for products and sales pages, and consulting related to SEO, lead generation, e-commerce optimization, and online funnels.

This pricing model carries both high risk and high reward. As you may recall, whoever takes the risk gets the upside.

I have never used the Performance-Based model, and I don't see that changing.

Here are the pros of the Performance-Based model:

APPENDIX

- The right clients and projects can make you a lot of money. Copywriter and marketing consultant Clayton Makepeace said he made up to $3 million in royalties each year.[5]

- This model removes friction from the sales process. The appeal of the Performance-Based model is easy to see. Clients pay little to nothing up front. They only pay you if you succeed, meaning that they pay you out of the revenues you generate for them. You take most of the risk on yourself, and in a way, you pay for yourself using the client's product or campaigns as your own revenue mechanism. What's not to like? Your confidence will be winsome, and you'll find it easier to close clients.

Here are the cons of the Performance-Based model:

- Attribution can be difficult. How much you make is tied to the sales or value created, and measuring your work's true impact can be very difficult. What if the client claims sales went up for other reasons? How are they handling attribution? What if the client doesn't have good analytics? What if they don't track the key numbers as closely as you'd like? To be successful with performance pricing, you and your client need to get crystal clear on how they will be measuring performance, how they will or won't attribute sales to your work, and how they will calculate your compensation. An unscrupulous client may promise you a percentage of gross revenue and later claim he said a percentage of net profit. My developmental editor, Amanda Lewis,

APPENDIX

has seen the Performance-Based model backfire on ghostwriters who cut a deal with the client for a percent of royalties. Later, the client bailed and didn't proceed with publishing. Guess who gets no royalties? The ghostwriter. Those nuances and details can be worth $10,000s. Spell them out clearly in your signed service agreements.

- Your upside may depend on other people's performance. It's one thing to stake your earning on your own skill and expertise. However, what if you stand to lose large sums when sales reps at your client's companies can't close the leads your new sales funnel produced for them? What if the ad manager's incompetence incinerates the ad budget without driving significant traffic to the sales page you wrote? Performance projects aren't a one-woman sport. To maximize upside, you need a whole team of A players. With this model the client invests in your performance, and you invest in their performance, too. Invest wisely.

- You must be really good. Your confidence in what your client is selling and your own ability to generate sales must be very high. Does your domain expertise make you highly desirable to this client? Do you have case studies that prove you can deliver results? Do you have a reputation? Do you have a proven process? If you can answer yes to those questions, you can hedge your downsides by asking for cash fees and a percentage of sales. Clayton Makepeace, who I mentioned earlier, was a legendary copywriter, and even he was extremely selective with the projects he accepted. I once stumbled

APPENDIX

across one of his intake questionnaires and was struck by how long, thorough, and specific it was. He obviously designed it to disqualify as many weak prospects as possible. He was one of the best in the world, and he was still cautious. A quote from Shane Parrish, the host of The Knowledge Project podcast and founder of Farnam Street, comes to mind: "While the rest of us are chasing brilliance, the best in the world know they must avoid stupidity before they can win."[6]

Positive Example: Consulting with Digital Agencies

In an interview, Viewability founder Tom Breeze explained how his YouTube ad agency uses performance pricing.[7]

Inbound leads come to Viewability pre-sold on the idea of not paying up front. The agency knows their formula for a good-fit client, and like Clayton Makepeace, they thoroughly qualify new prospects before starting the initial four- to six-week test, one that Viewability pays for.

By the third month, most campaigns are profitable for the client, and Breeze said 80 percent of Viewability's clients end up being a win for the agency. Performance pricing costs more for some clients, but they get the results they want and are happy.

Closing Thoughts on Pricing Models

Let's finish where we started: There is no one-size-fits-all approach to pricing. You should let the project pick the pricing

APPENDIX

model, and as you estimate a project's price, recognize that you're running a calculation of time and risk:

- Will the client be a lazy communicator and force you to decipher confusing messages?
- Will the original scope stay more or less the same?
- Will the client need a lot of hand holding?
- Will he change his mind a dozen times?
- Will she go mid-project?

A complex project is like a bucket with the potential for a dozen small leaks. The bigger the scope and longer the timeline, the higher the risk of time lost. When you lose time, your effective hourly rate goes down.

What matters more than the type of pricing is a paradigm shift. Smart freelancers sell outcomes, not hours. They're conscious of which party is taking on more risk in the project. They may start a new client on one pricing model and later switch to another.

The right pricing model is the one that minimizes risk, maximizes your revenue (rather, your EHR), and strengthens your positioning. Each project that you sell at or near your Dream Rate gets you that much closer to your target income and the freelance lifestyle you want.

NOTES

Introduction

[1] Joe Rogan and Bryan Callen, "Deer the Hard Way: Prince of Wales Island," Meat Eater S 05, Ep. 03, (Jan. 21, 2015). https://www.themeateater.com/shows/meateater/season-5/deer-the-hard-way-prince-of-wales-island-joe-rogan-and-bryan-callen; Erin Strout, "What is 'Type II' Fun, and Why do Some People Want to Have It?" *Washington Post*, (Mar. 24, 2022). https://www.washingtonpost.com/wellness/2022/03/24/what-is-type-2-fun. As far as I can tell, the fun scale originated in 1985 with Rainer Newberry, a geology professor at the University of Alaska. He shared the concept with geologist and climber Peter Haeussler, who shared it with climber Kelly Cordes, who wrote a piece about it, which Matt Samet later edited for *Climbing* magazine. Samet then included the fun scale in his book, *Climbing Dictionary: Mountaineering Slang, Terms, Neologisms & Lingo*, and it eventually found its way into the cultural lexicon of climbers and other people with a penchant for Type II fun.

Move One

[1] Charles Dickens, "*Hunted Down,*" *Hard Times and Reprinted Pieces*, (London: Chapman & Hall, 1905), 4.

NOTES

Move Three

[1] Calin Ciabi, "The Real Cost of Living in Cebu, Philippines," *Nomad, Not Mad*, (Jan. 10, 2023). https://nomadnotmad.com/the-real-cost-of-living-in-cebu-philippines.

[2] Dr. Benjamin Hardy, "Introduction," *Be Your Future Self Now*, (Hay House, 2022), xxxiv.

Move Four

[1] Beth Longman, "Couldn't resist posting this conversation with a local marketing agency owner," LinkedIn. https://www.linkedin.com/posts/beth-longman_freelancerrates-freelancing-freelancecopywriter-activity-6957717127860527105-ZpaJ.

[2] Chris Voss, *Never Split the Difference: Negotiating As If Your Life Depended On It*, (New York: Harper Business, 2016), 133.

[3] A. de Berker, R. Rutledge, C. Mathys, et al, "Computations of Uncertainty Mediate Acute Stress Responses in Humans," *Nature Communications* 7, (2016). https://www.nature.com/articles/ncomms10996.

[4] C. Camerer and M. Weber, "Recent Developments in Modeling Preferences: Uncertainty and Ambiguity," *Journal of Risk and Uncertainty* 5, (1992): 325–370. https://link.springer.com/article/10.1007/BF00122575.

[5] A large body of empirical psychological research supports this idea of ambiguity aversion and the Ellsberg Paradox. If that rabbit hole interests you, start with the Wikipedia pages for Ambiguity Aversion and Ellsberg Paradox.

NOTES

[6] Benjamin Hardy and Dan Sullivan, *The Gap and The Gain: The High Achievers' Guide to Happiness, Confidence, and Success* (New York: Hay House Business, 2021).

[7] Jesse Koepke (@jessekoepkecuts). "If your rate isn't rejected, add 10% to your next project." (Twitter, Jun. 28, 2022, 9:02 a.m.). https://twitter.com/jessekoepkecuts/status/1541784055276085250.

Move Five

[1] Rachel, "AMA with Austin Church" Pollen, (May 9, 2023). https://app.runpollen.com/community/c/announcements/ama-with-austin-church-on-tuesday-may-9th-post-your-questions-ahead-of-time.

[2] Nathan Barry, "The Ladders of Wealth Creation: A Step-by-Step Roadmap to Building Wealth," (Dec. 3, 2019). https://nathanbarry.com/wealth-creation/

[3] Kevin Kelley and Shane Parrish, *The Knowledge Project*, Ep. 166, Farnam Street Media. https://fs.blog/knowledge-project-podcast/kevin-kelly.

[4] Jim Collins and Jerry I. Porras, Built to Last: Successful Habits of Visionary Companies , (New York: Harper Business, 1994), https://www.jimcollins.com/concepts/bhag.html.

[5] Nail Gaiman, "Make Good Art." University of the Arts, Philadelphia. (2012) https://www.uarts.edu/makegoodart.

NOTES

⁶ Cameron Herold. *Vivid Vision: A Remarkable Tool for Aligning Your Business around a Shared Vision of the Future*, (Austin: Lioncrest Publishing, 2020), 34.

Move Six

¹ J. K. Rowling, "The Fringe Benefits of Failure, and the Importance of Imagination," *The Harvard Gazette*, (2008), https://news.harvard.edu/gazette/story/2008/06/text-of-j-k-rowling-speech.

² Paul B. Batalden, Eugene C. Nelson, Marjorie M. Godfrey, et al. *Quality By Design: A Clinical Microsystems Approach*, (San Francisco: Jossey-Bass, 2007), 205. This quote has mutated over time. It's often attributed to engineer and management consultant W. Edwards Deming, but the best trail of breadcrumbs leads back to one of his colleagues, Dr. Paul Batalden, who likely borrowed the idea from organizational design expert Arthur W. Jones: "All organizations are perfectly designed to get the results they get!" In a book he co-authored, Quality By Design: A Clinical Microsystems Approach, Batalden says the quote came from personal communication to Donald Berwick, IHI President and CEO, in 1996.

³ Carl Jung, "Christ: A Symbol of the Self," *Aion: Researches into the Phenomenology of the Self* (New York: Routledge, 1991), 70–71.

⁴ History.com Editors, "Roger Bannister Runs First Four-Minute Mile," (A&E Television Networks, May 4, 2020), https://www.history.com/this-day-in-history/first-four-minute-mile; Wikipedia contributors, "Mile run world

NOTES

record progression," *Wikipedia, The Free Encyclopedia*, https://en.wikipedia.org/w/index.php?title=Mile_run_world_record_progression&oldid=1185580200; Steve Magness, "The Roger Bannister Effect: The Myth of the Psychological Breakthrough," The Science of Running, https://www.scienceofrunning.com/2017/05/the-roger-bannister-effect-the-myth-of-the-psychological-breakthrough.html?v=47e5dceea252; Matt Frazier, "What We Mortals Can Learn from the 4-Minute Mile," No Meat Athlete, https://www.nomeatathlete.com/4-minute-mile-certainty.

[5] Wikipedia contributors, "We choose to go to the Moon," *Wikipedia, The Free Encyclopedia*, https://en.wikipedia.org/w/index.php?title=We_choose_to_go_to_the_Moon&oldid=1174100728.

[6] Marie Poulin, "Earning $40,000 Per Month as a Course Creator," Creator Science, Ep. 78, https://podcast.creatorscience.com/marie-poulin.

[7] Josh Hall, "Price Is Not the Problem: The Fool-Proof Way to Price Projects" Creator Science, Workshop with Josh Hall. https://lab.creatorscience.com/c/workshops/pricing-is-not-your-problem.

[8] Alex Hormozi, "This ONE Thing Will Make You a Better Entrepreneur," (YouTube, Sept. 20, 2022), https://youtu.be/JsXZzgD_k9k.

[9] B. Klontz, S. L. Britt, J. Mentzer, & T. Klontz, "Money Beliefs and Financial Behaviors: Development of the Klontz

NOTES

Money Script Inventory," *Journal of Financial Therapy*, 2 (1) 1, (2011). https://doi.org/10.4148/jft.v2i1.451.

[10] T. Rowe Price, "10th Annual Parents, Kids & Money Survey", Slideshare, (May 19, 2018), https://www.slideshare.net/TRowePrice/t-rowe-prices-10th-annual-parents-kids-money-survey.

[11] Daniel Thomas, "Who Is Elizabeth Holmes and Why Was She On Trial," British Broadcasting Company (Nov. 18, 2022), https://www.bbc.com/news/business-58336998.

[12] Patagonia, "One Percent for the Planet," Patagonia.com, https://www.patagonia.com/one-percent-for-the-planet.html.

[13] David Gelles, "Billionaire No More: Patagonia Founder Gives Away the Company," *The New York Times*, (Sept. 14, 2022), https://www.nytimes.com/2022/09/14/climate/patagonia-climate-philanthropy-chouinard.html.

[14] Eudie Pak, "The Many Wives of Ernest Hemingway," Biography.com (Apr. 6, 2021), https://www.biography.com/authors-writers/ernest-hemingway-wives.

[15] Eric Meisfjord, "The Truth about Ernest Hemingway's Many Wives," Grunge.com, (Mar. 2, 2023), https://www.grunge.com/188914/the-truth-about-ernest-hemingways-many-wives.

[16] Robert Tomasson, "Hemingway Estate $1.4 Million; Widow Is His Lone Beneficiary," The New York Times (Feb. 22, 1964). https://archive.nytimes.com/www.nytimes.com/books/99/07/04/specials/hemingway-estate.html; Andrea di

NOTES

Robilant, "Papa the Investor," *The Paris Review*, (Mar. 4, 2017). https://www.theparisreview.org/blog/2017/03/24/papa-the-investor.

[17] Ryan Holiday, "James Clear on Getting 1% Better daily with Stoicism," Daily Stoic, (Mar. 1, 2021). https://youtu.be/0QKd-ulbH5E?t=2912.

[18] Ibid.

[19] Andy J. Pizza, "This 4 Part Creative Practice Plan Took Me from Frantic to focused in 15 Minutes," Creative Pep Talk, Ep. 375, (Aug 3, 2022). https://www.creativepeptalk.com/375-this-4-part-creative-practice-plan-took-me-from-from-frantic-to-focused-in-15-minutes.

[20] Review of *The Lives of Danielle Steel: The Unauthorized Biography of America's #1 Best-Selling Author*, Publishersweekly.com, (Oct 1994). (Retrieved Nov 13, 2017).

[21] Morgan Housel, *The Psychology of Money: Timeless Lessons on Wealth, Greed, and Happiness*, (London: Harriman House, 2021).

[22] Olivia Goldhill, "Neuroscience Confirms That To Be Tuly Happy, You Will Always Need Something More," Quartz, (May 15, 2016). https://qz.com/684940/neuroscience-confirms-that-to-be-truly-happy-you-will-always-need-something-more.

[23] P. Brickman, D. Coates, & R. Janoff-Bulman, (1978). Lottery winners and accident victims: Is happiness relative? *Journal of Personality and Social Psychology*, 36(8), 917–927. https://doi.org/10.1037/0022-3514.36.8.917.

NOTES

[24] Dan Gilbert, "The Surprising Science of Happiness," TED (Feb 2004). https://www.ted.com/talks/dan_gilbert_the_surprising_science_of_happiness

[25] Sonja Lyubomirsky. *The How of Happiness: A New Approach to Getting the Life You Want*. (New York: Penguin Press, 2007).

[26] Philippians 4:11–12. *The Holy Bible*, English Standard Version. (Crossway, 2001).

[27] Acharya Buddharakkhita, trans. "verse 204," *The Dhammapada: The Buddha's Path to Wisdom*, (1996).

[28] Jennifer Robison, "Happiness Is Love—and $75,000," *Business Journal* (Gallup, Nov 17, 2011). https://news.gallup.com/businessjournal/150671/happiness-is-love-and-75k.aspx.

[29] Daniel Kahneman and Angus Deaton, "High income improves evaluation of life but not emotional well-being," PNAS Vol 107, No. 38 (Sept 7, 2010). https://doi.org/10.1073/pnas.1011492107.

[30] The Ascent Staff, "It Pays to Be Generous," The Ascent (Motley Fool, Oct 27, 2021). https://www.fool.com/the-ascent/research/study-it-pays-be-generous/#:~:text=High%2Dgenerosity%20people%20were%2023,%2C%20their%20possessions%2C%20and%20more.

[31] Ibid, 22.

NOTES

Move Seven

[1] Glenn Allsopp, "The 122Bn SEO Industry: 31 Success Stories (with Revenue Numbers) for 2023," Detailed. https://gaps.com/seo-industry.

See also https://casestudybuddy.com.

[2] Brad Smith, "How Joel Klettke's Case Study Buddy Scales Revenue—Generating SaaS Testimonials" Codeless, (Jun. 17, 2019). https://codeless.io/joel-klettke.

[3] Harvey S. Firestone and Shane Parrish, *Men and Rubber: The Story of Business*. (Latticework Publishing, 2023).

[4] Derek Sivers, Hell Yeah or No: What's Worth Doing, (Hit Media, 2020).

[5] Alex Hormozi (@AlexHormozi), "Selling is a transference of belief over a bridge of trust." (Twitter, Aug. 19, 2022, 7:40 a.m.). https://twitter.com/AlexHormozi/status/1560607565481926656.

[6] Caroline Davies and Michael Paterson, "BP Attacked over 136m Logo as Petrol Prices Soar," *The Telegraph*, (July 25, 2000). https://www.telegraph.co.uk/news/uknews/1350238/BP-attacked-over-136m-logo-as-petrol-prices-soar.html.

[7] Doug Evans, "1993 Interview re: Paul Rand and Steve Jobs," (YouTube, Jan 7, 2007). https://www.youtube.com/watch?v=xb8idEf-Iak.

[8] Herman Melville, "Hawthorne and His Mosses," *The Literary World* (New York, Aug. 1850).

NOTES

Move Eight

[1] Jonathan Stark, "Outrageous Prices," Email Newsletter, (Jun. 12, 2021). https://jonathanstark.com/daily/20210612-1740-outrageous-prices.

[2] *The Brothers Bloom*, directed by Rian Johnson, (Summit Entertainment, 2008).

[3] Gary C. Halbert, "Chapter 6," *The Boron Letters*. https://thegaryhalbertletter.com/Boron/TChapter6.htm

[4] Ed Gandia, Personal Correspondence.

Appendix

[1] Jonathan Stark, "Outrageous Prices," Email Newsletter, (Jun. 12, 2021). https://jonathanstark.com/daily/20210612-1740-outrageous-prices.

[2] Oprah Winfrey, "Oprah Recalls One of Her Favorite Life Lessons from Maya Angelou," Oprah's Lifeclass, OWN, (YouTube, Oct. 27, 2011). https://m.youtube.com/watch?v=BTiziwBhd54.

[3] "The Business Model Canvas," Strategyzer. https://www.strategyzer.com/canvas/business-model-canvas.

[4] David Baker and Chris Do, "Why I Started to Charge 10K Per Day—The Whole Story," The Futur, (YouTube, Apr. 30, 2020). https://www.youtube.com/watch?v=HbKnXeZAXoU&feature=youtu.be.

NOTES

[5] Will Newman, "The Story Behind the Highest-Paid Copywriter Today and What He Can Tell You About Achieving," *The Writer's Life*, (American Writers and Artists Institute, June 13, 2016). https://www.awai.com/2016/06/story-behind-highest-paid-copywriter-today.

[6] "Adult Life," *Brain Food* 546, Farnam Street Media, (Oct. 15, 2023). https://fs.blog/brain-food/october-15-2023.

[7] Jason Swenk, "How Can an Agency Implement a Performance-Based Pricing Model," Jasonswenk.com, (Mar. 23, 2016). https://jasonswenk.com/performance-based-pricing.

ACKNOWLEDGEMENTS

My fascination with getting better results with less effort led me here, to my first book, a pricing and money mindset guide. I didn't see that coming until it made a whole lot of sense, and many people deserve recognition and gratitude for nudging me along. (You'll have to start the music to get me off the stage.)

Chuck Morris, you gave a young poet fresh out of grad school and dewy with idealism and literary pretensions his first job in marketing. Thanks for rolling the dice on me.

Andrew Gordon, you taught me my enduring first lesson as a freelancer: pricing is branding. Thank you for convincing me to take myself seriously and raise my prices so that I could be taken more seriously as a result.

Thanks to my many freelance and consulting clients over the last fifteen years. My baseline hope was always to do no harm, and my ambition was to leave each of you in a much better position than I found you. Thank you for putting your trust and dollars in me. Any resemblance between yourselves and characters in this book of nonfiction is purely coincidental.

Thanks to the many people who have shaped my thinking about money and my relationship to it: Mariah Coz, Morgan Housel, Ramit Sethi, Nick True, Andy J. Pizza, Jonathan Stark, Jay Clouse, Chris Do, Denise Duffield-Thomas, and many

ACKNOWLEDGEMENTS

others I'm undoubtedly forgetting. Thanks to Chris Guillebeau and David Fugate for putting out *The Unconventional Guide to Publishing* back in 2012. You helped me find my way. Thanks to Rob Fitzpatrick for your book, *Write Useful Books*. It was exceedingly, uh, useful.

Thanks to the beta readers who gave me honest feedback on the outline before I'd written a word of the book: Deanne Topping, Kelly Steele, Emily Mills, and Jay Sennett. And thanks to all the folks who shared the stories and perspectives that found their way into the final manuscript. Without a doubt this book would be more ponderous and less helpful without your input and honesty.

Thanks to the everyone who pre-ordered the book and put a little pep in my step: Arne, Art, Bob, Britt, Chris, Cynthia, David, Delphine, Elizabeth, Evan, Ezekiel, Jeannine, Kim, Leah, Linda, Matt, Paul, Petar, Rachel (Boller), Rachel (Smith), Richard, Sharon, Suzie, Teresa, and Trevor.

Daren Smith and Steph Smith, you encouraged me to snap out of my overthinking (translation: stupor) and finish the first manuscript by writing it in public.

Ed Gandia and Ilise Benun, you sharpened my thinking and wrote blurbs. Thank you.

Thank you to my developmental editor, Amanda Lewis. You convinced an ugly duckling it was a swan. Thanks to my line editor, Steve Woodward, for camaraderie near the finish line and superb janitorial services.

ACKNOWLEDGEMENTS

Thanks to my assistant, Bern, for tracking down original sources and citations, fact checking, and doing innumerable other tasks that helped to free me up so that I could finish the durn thing.

Thanks to Matt Briel, Sarah Gilbert, and the rest of the team at Tilt Publishing and Lulu Press.

Thank you to my wife Megan for the encouragement and unfailing support. You took on more than your fair share of kid duty while I spent Saturdays here and there pushing this project over whatever obstacle it faced at the time. You're my ride or die.

Thank you, Jesus. You told me I'm here on earth to help people get free, and this book is one expression of that calling. I'll spend the rest of eternity thanking you for the freedom you have given me.

To every person who bought and read this book, thank you for your time and vote of confidence. May this book return a hundred and a thousand times more than you invested, and may you be in a better position to bankroll your freedom and bring freedom to others

January 2024

ABOUT THE AUTHOR

Ever since I can remember, I have wanted to write books. Well, that's not precisely true. The life plan I wrote down in first grade included living in a mansion, marrying a girl at church named Jordan, and being a "sientist."

"Sientists" spent their time outside turning over rocks in creeks and sneaking in some fishing, or so I thought. That sounded good to me. Thirty years later, I'm still turning over rocks, only instead of crayfish and hellgrammites, I look for patterns, principles, and processes. I'm still eager to talk about what I discovered with anyone who will listen. Books are better suited than "sience" for that.

When I'm not writing, I masquerade as a marketing leader and freelance coach. I started freelancing in 2009 after finishing my MA in Literature and getting laid off from a marketing agency. Freelancing accidentally became my career. Along the way, I've taken several scenic detours, including a portfolio of mobile apps, a tech startup, a children's book (*Grabbling*), and a branding studio.

My wife and I live with our three children in Knoxville, Tennessee. They put up with my many fascinations, including running, barbeque, fly fishing, entrepreneurship, and what I'll loosely call "leverage."

I love teaching freelancers, consultants, and creators how to stack up specific advantages and find their income-lifestyle sweet spot. You can learn more at FreelanceCake.com.